Unleashed Chains

Based on a True Story

BY:

HAZEL

Unleashed Chains

-A Novel Written By-

Hazel

Copyright © 2017 by Author Hazel

Published by Author Hazel

Facebook: Author Hazel

Cover Design: Angel Walker

ACKNOWLEDGEMENTS

To my children, Alfrado, Bria, Brian, and Devin. Thanks for being a valuable part of my life and believing in me. Thank you for believing in me to lead and guide you towards God by the discipline that I exemplified.

~Mommy will always love each of you to life~

To my Mother, Henrine Smith. Thank you for continuing to empower me with my life's challenges. I love you more than words itself.

~Thank you~

To my Father, William Smith Jr (RIH). Thank you for showing me how to be an entrepreneur. I'm told often that I am a go getter just like you were.

~I miss you, but know I will see you again~

To my Sisters and Brothers, Shawn Wells, Joseph Peyton, Tawona C. Smith, William L. Smith, William Smith III, Christopher Smith, Willie Marquis (William Smith IV), and Felicia Smith. Thank you all for the individual time we share. You all have touched my life in one way or another.

~From the Jack of all Trades~

To my Nieces and Nephews, Brandi, Mya, Gabrielle, Brandon, William, Bryce, and Waylon. Thank each of you for keeping me abreast of my youthful side.

~Auntie loves each of you~

Thanks to my Aunt Mary, Aunt Thelma, and Aunt Juanita. Thank you all for showing me love and support during my time of adolescence.

~I love you all~

Thanks to my Uncles, George (Uddie), William Henry, and Uncle Joe. Thank you all for showing me love and support.

~Love Vee~

*To my Cousins, Joey, Tondra, Joe
(Sport), Angel, Anthony, Marcus, and
Christopher (Carvail). Thank you all
for the support and believing in me.*

~Flashback, I love you all~

*To my Grandma, Annie B Wells
(Walls). Thank you for showing me
love and always making me laugh.
Thank you for showing me how to be
a strong woman and always giving
me advice to make it through my
trials.*

*~I miss you so much Grandma. You live in my
heart forever. Love your Granddaughter Vee~*

Thanks to my friend and Counselor, Centrell Sutton. Thank you for continuing to be here for me, no matter the outcome and the disagreements we've encountered. Thank you for keeping me grounded in the roughest of times. Thank you for the encouraging words and actions.

~I am truly Blessed to have a friend like you~

I would like to say how grateful I am to everyone who I did not name, who has touched my life in some way or another. I wish I could name each of you, but you all know exactly who you are. To my cousins, Michelle Brown, Sondra Shields, and Toya Lucas, just to name a couple.

~Thank you all so much for just being there~

About the Author

First let me start off by telling you a little bit about myself. My name is Lavenda Smith. I received my name from my father, who named me after his mother. I was born to the parents of William and Henrine, in Memphis TN. I am a single parent mother of four wonderful children. I graduated from a Private High School located in Tennessee. In 1995, I went off to a two year college, located in Mississippi. I am the Sole Proprietor of DABB ENTERPRISE, that I

started four years ago, from my home.

My children motivate me. Therefore, I

named my small business after them;

I also started an in home child care in

2006, God's Image Covered Child

Care (GICCC). I've been a Poet since

the age of five. Anytime I experience

something, I keep a journal of it. I am

a Published Passionate Author and

Poet. I take everything I do seriously,

especially when it comes to praising

God, raising my children, and helping others. I am very passionate about God's people. I have been through a lot and my journey in trials and tribulations are not over yet until my spirit is called to glory. My life experiences have taught me how to be humble. God has always known me, and I'm so glad He did. Had He taken His hands off me, I would be one lost soul.

TABLE OF CONTENTS

Inspirational..................................... 19

Introduction.................................... 33

Scripture... 42

Chapter One-

The Lavish Life................................ 43

Chapter Two-

Evicted... 65

Chapter Three-

Separation..................................... 77

Chapter Four-

New Home....................................... 87

Chapter Five-

Pool Time... 95

Chapter Six-

Molestation...................................... 103

Chapter Seven-

A Funny Feeling................................ 115

Chapter Eight-

Secret Revealed................................. 121

Chapter Nine-

Drunken Behavior.............................. 143

Chapter Ten-

Two Perverted Men............................ 153

Chapter Eleven-

School Time..................................... 167

Chapter Twelve-

My Journal.................................... 185

Chapter Thirteen-

Unknown Anger.............................. 193

Chapter Fourteen-

The Day I've Waited For...................... 205

Chapter Fifteen-

Accident Prone................................ 217

Chapter Sixteen-

Acting Out of Resentment.................... 233

Chapter Seventeen-

Confession of My Sins......................... 247

Chapter Eighteen-

Break-In.................................... 261

Chapter Nineteen-

Grandma's House............................. 271

Chapter Twenty-

Neighborhood Friends........................ 283

Chapter Twenty-One-

Talent and Popularity........................ 291

Chapter Twenty-Two-

The P Game.................................. 297

Chapter Twenty-Three-

Power in the Tongue......................... 303

Chapter Twenty-Four-

Class Clown................................. 307

Chapter Twenty-Five-

Bullying...................................... 315

Chapter Twenty-Six-

Anna and Marcus........................... 323

Chapter Twenty-Seven-

My Father's New Family................... 331

Chapter Twenty-Eight-

To Be Continued........................... 343

INSPIRATIONAL

In life, we all have been
through or going through some things
that we may feel will shame our lives.
Some of us are bound by the
generational curses on our lives as we
have become adults. There are some
circumstances that have occurred in
our life that has silence us to not
speak up. We have been silenced to
the place of not having a voice. We all

have a story to tell. Some are good, not so good, bad, good and bad, and indifferent, but we all have gone or going through something in our lives. It's what we choose to do with what has taken place in our own lives that will give us the freedom to break the chains or stay bound to the enemy tricks. Our book is being written. God doesn't allow us to go through the unknown for Him to bring us out and not testify about how He brought us out. We are to share our coming out to

those who are suffering from what
God has already delivered us from, to
help them see Christ in their
tribulations so that their faith will be
made whole. Our test is not in vain.
Our test was not meant to be kept a
secret.

Some of us have been molested,
raped, abused, talked about, falsely
accused of things that did not take
place, addicted to drugs, addicted to
sex, habitual liars, thieves, murders,
and lied on. Most of us are still being

molested, raped, sexually assaulted, and talked about, and so on. Some of us have experienced several of the above sins, but that doesn't make us less than anyone. We have all sinned and fallen short of the Glory of God. God still love us. God chastises those of whom He loves. For God so loved the world, that He gave His Only Begotten Son, that whosoever believeth in Him should not perish, but have everlasting life (John 3:16 KJV). He gives us a free will to choose to love Him and follow after Him. Why can't we offer a sacrifice unto The LORD as He sacrificed His Only Begotten Son for us? When you seek after God's face, He will show you the way. When you ask for forgiveness, He throws your sin into the lake of forgiveness and don't look back. You see, God is the same God today, as He was yesterday, and will be forever more. The list can go on and on! When we choose to take a stand and fight the cause, our life will turn around and the burden will be lifted. If we study God's word and connect to his Holy Spirit, He will guide us to the area that speaks to our own personal lives. It's good to share your test in life that will help save someone who may be experiencing the very same thing God has delivered you from.

Everyone experience things differently in their own lives. Even though we may go through the same thing, the experience is totally different. Some of us have mentors

who can help guide us through our

hardship, disappointments, setbacks,

and letdowns. Some of us may not see

a way out of those very same issues,

because we have no support system.

No matter the circumstances, through

Christ we can conquer anything.

There's no limit to what God can and

will do. The very same thing you see

as a hindrance, may look that way, but

will actually turn out to be your

deliverance. You have to look at it in

every aspect of your life. Why is this happening to me? What is ahead that will turn this situation in my life to a testimony? Am I following after God's will for my life? Am I seeking God for the answers to my situation? Am I trying to figure it out on my own that is causing more friction and a delayed response from God?

We should become more positive to the negative to create a more prominent life that reflects our Creator, Heavenly Father. When we begin to accept the things in our lives and seek God for a positive outlook and allow Him to walk with us through our journey, we will get a better result and God's will for our lives we become known. In doing this, we will overcome every obstacle no matter good or bad.

I have a voice, you have a voice, and we all have a voice. Use it to help save someone from hurt, turmoil, abuse, addiction, or whatever the experience you have encountered that you have now been set free from, to help them become free. It's okay to speak up and speak out. Your test is the reason you have a testimony. Be released and tap into the spirit that will take you to a place of connecting with the Father. We all need our own personal relationship with The Father. When you develop a personal relationship with Him, He will speak directly to you. Having a personal relationship with The Father will give you a better aspect on life and what

His plans are for your life. Connect with Him and it will restore the faith you have within yourself to solely depend on Him for all things. Of course, The Father speaks to you on different levels, through different people, and through different circumstances. He does not speak to each one of us the same, therefore it is imperative for you to connect with Him personally. When you're spiritually connected with The Father, you'll be able to hear Him clearly.

Only your connection with The Father will become prominent in your life, as you continue to receive Him. Listen for God's direction. When you find yourself in a situation that you feel you can't come out of, seek God's face and wait on His response. Sometimes we try to figure things out ourselves, but we end up falling into a deeper ditch than where we started. Why is this so? We tried to do it on our own, instead of seeking The Father for the answers. The battle is not ours to fight, leave it to God to

protect us and He will conquer it all.

Ask yourself these questions:

Why did Jesus die for me? Was I

worth dying for? Do I deserve to be

where I am today? How did I get to

this journey? Do I really give God the

Glory for the many blessings He's

poured into my bosom, or am I taking

the credit for something that I cannot

create in my own image? Am I where

I should be? What are the stumbling

blocks that are keeping me from reaching my goals?

When you begin to evaluate your own personal life, and equip yourself with the power and knowledge coming from God, your life will begin to transform to a much better place.

Introduction

In this story, you will find a

little girl who struggles growing up.

She was an outcast, she was

neglected, belittled, mentally and

verbally abused by her biological

parent, as well as other people close

to her, and those she let into her heart.

She had a big heart and loved to help

anyone. The divorce of her parents

and the twisted things her father

partook in, made it even more difficult for her to focus in school and learn how not to trust people around her. As she went through the motions of her childhood, she was faced with the bondage and generational curses that followed her, which led to her own broken friendships she tried developing with the people who surrounded her. These generational curses were relinquished on her life because she didn't have the knowledge to connect her to The Holy

Spirit, at such a young age. The Holy Spirit is the source of life that is so important to help guide her through life's challenges, but she wasn't taught about this source. She had no one to teach her. Her mother was so focused on her own life that she didn't realize she was destroying her own children lives. Did her mom realize she was hurting her own children, or was it because she was hurt she wanted everyone around her to suffer too? Or was it that her mom went through so much turmoil in her own life and that she didn't know any other way but to be the way she is?

This little girl grew up in a home where her mother kept her sheltered from the outside world, which made it hard for her to function later in life. The challenges that she was faced with as a little girl, was once the position of her mother, her grandmother's, her aunts, and her cousins too. This curse has trickle down from generation to generation,

until one day she began tapping into
her inner spirit and finding her way
through Jesus Christ, our Lord and
Savior. It was because God knew her
and didn't take His hands off her life,
the reason she's able to seek Christ
and allow Him to lead and guide her
through her challenges of life.
Through her inner spirit she was led
by the Holy Spirit into the unknown.
She realized that one day, she had to
break and relinquish the generational
curses off her own life, so that she

wouldn't live in bondage and pass this same curse to her children and children's children.

As you read this story, think about your own life. Are there any chains that still have you bound today? Have all curses been unleashed from your life? What have you done different in your child or children lives that wasn't done right in your life? Do you have a spiritual connection with the Father? Are you still living the life you were living as a child? Have you allowed The Father to show you the gifts He has for your life to help guide someone else from continuing a path The Father directed you out of?

Look back on your life, and find that hurtful area that kept you bound. Where are you today with that same issue? Is God getting the glory from your story? Or do you feel like you conquered something on your own?

Sometimes we as adults feel we are setting good examples and living the life we think we should be living.

Often time, we don't realize the pain we are inflicting on ourselves and our loved ones surrounding us. If we really sit and observe our individual lives, we may find that we have adapted to the environment that we grew up in, but fail to adjust to what's right in the eye sight of God.

If we don't develop that personal relationship with The Father for ourselves, we will continue to fall victim to the bondage of having a mindset that we are not worthy of

God. Think about it, every Pastor,

Minister, Evangelist, and so on who

say they were called by God are

sinners too, just as you are. This is not

to discredit anyone and doesn't mean

that God has not brought them out of

a situation, this is just waking you up

to acknowledge that you are

somebody and you are loved by

Christ, just as the head of the church

is loved by Christ.

Mathew 6:33 KJV

*But seek ye first the kingdom
of God, and His righteousness;
and all these things shall be
added unto you.*

Chapter One
The Lavish Life

It all began back in the year of 1979, in the beautiful city, City of the Blues and Rock and Roll, Memphis Tennessee, where I was born. The city is on the border of Arkansas and Mississippi. I'm small, country, very active and a spoiled child. By all accounts I am a beautiful child, flawless light skin complexion, sandy brown hair with hazel eyes which changed with my mood. I am my father's, baby girl and last pea in the pod; at least that was for the moment. As many children as my father already had, who knows what other child or children was going to pop up next. Even though my father had a lot of children, he didn't make a difference in us he loved us all the same. I looked up to him and loved him with all my heart, he is my hero.

I have always thought highly of my father. The material things that my father had in his possession, made me

realized that he had accomplished so

much in his life. Because of all the

things he had accumulated in his life,

I felt that we were rich and had

everything a child could ever dream

of. I felt this way because he had the

finest of things: things such as; an

expensive car with the built-in phone,

a large variety of expensive jewelry,

shoes, clothes, and much more than I

or anyone could ever imagine,

especially knowing the circumstances

behind his career. We lived in a big, red, brick house, with upstairs and downstairs, with a yard about the size of a football field. It was my father Major Jr., my mother Asiana, my sister Clover, my brother Major Lee, and I, who lived in the big house. My mother is a Nurse who traveled with my father, quite often. My father was born in a beautiful small town outside of New Madrid. My grandparents are Major Sr. and Sandy. My father is the only child. He stayed in Missouri for a while and then went on to live in Chi-Town after my paternal grandmother transitioned into eternal life. He worked on the police force in Chicago and obtained several businesses during his stay. He served as a body guard and FBI agent in the early 1970's. He owned a limousine company and gas station. Later, he moved to Memphis, where he then served as an undercover police officer for Memphis Housing Authority, as a Narcotic Officer for Memphis Police

Department, and as a Shelby County Deputy Sheriff Officer. My father took much pride in performing his daily duties as a provider for our home and an enforcement officer for the citizens of our city. My father was well-known and established.

My mother was born in Mississippi. She was the first child of five. She lived in Mississippi for quite some time. She also conceived five children, to which I was the fifth and last child. She then met my father and began traveling back and forth, from Missouri, to Chicago, to New York, and several other places. She became the fifth wife to my father. She conceived children with my father.

My mother wasn't able to continue pursuing her career in Nursing because of the big break-up between her and my father. She gave up everything to gain her own identity back. My father stripped my mother. She loved him so much but he took her love for granted and remained the man that he really was covering up.

It's funny, because I do not ever recall seeing any fights or hearing any arguments between my parents. Maybe my mom stayed in the kitchen a lot because my father demanded her to cook his meals. My father didn't know how to cook. But who knows, because I was only a little girl and didn't notice any abnormal behavior between my parents, maybe they designed it to be that way so that it

wouldn't affect our livelihood. All I
remember are a lot of good moments.
I remember my mother cooking
family meals and inviting family to
come over and have dinner with us. I
remember the times when we would
all sit around the big, oval shaped,
brown kitchen table as a family and
have family discussions. My brother
Major Lee and I would go outside and
play in the yard together while
chasing our dog. We named our dog,
New York. This name was given to

him because our mother would travel a lot to New York City, with our father. He was an adorable, small, white poodle with nice curly hair.

I was such a mean three year, little old girl, well, that's what I was told. I was very active. I would always chase and bite the tail of our dog New York. One day I was trying to play with New York, I picked him up and bit his tail, because he wanted to jump down out of my arms. I didn't know that because I bit his tail it would be the last time I would bite him again. New York jumped out of my arms, whining as he ran off down the street. New York ran away and never came back. Everyone was sad about New York running away, except for me. After all, I was the reason he ran away.

I never got into any serious trouble, but I am a busy body, always doing dangerous things. I am so spoil and I get my way with just about anything, I especially get my way with my father. My father will not allow anyone to spank me, but my brother Major Lee get spankings every now and again. I don't recall my sister Clover getting into any trouble. She is always the quiet one. She likes to do a lot of excessive posing for the camera, picture perfect. She stays out of the way of everyone. You won't even notice she's around, that's how quiet and soft spoken she is.

One day my brother Major Lee and I were playing and running

throughout the house. Major Lee had to take a potty break so he stopped by the downstairs bathroom and took a leak. For some reason my father was upset and was headed to the bathroom, but Major Lee was using it with the door open. My father entered the bathroom, went over toward Major Lee and started whooping him. As I stood by the bathroom door, I watched Major Lee utilizing the toilet and our father standing behind him whooping him for peeing in the toilet.

I was afraid and wondered, why is he whooping my brother for doing what he is supposed to be doing? My father kept saying, you should've closed the door when using the bathroom and you know you are not supposed to be using this bathroom without permission. I couldn't understand, as a little girl, what my brother had done so wrong to get a whooping. This is the only incident I witnessed. I felt sad for my brother as he stood there crying trying to hold his urine. Our mother came out of nowhere and

asked our father, "MAJOR!! What in

the hell is wrong with you? Why are

you beating on him like that?" The

look on my father's face was a look

that only an angry man would give

someone he's about to go to war with.

My father shook his head, yelled at

my mother, and said, "HE SHOULD

HAVE CLOSED THE DOOR

WHILE USING THE DAMN

BATHROOM!" And my father

walked passed my mother, with his

fist balled up, biting on his bottom lip, starred at her with this evil look as if he wanted to knock her the hell out, and then he slowly walked out the bathroom, with his shoulders pushed back as if he was the toughest man that ever walked the face of the earth. My mother walked over to my brother and hugged him while whispering to him, 'Major Lee, everything will be alright and don't worry, you didn't do anything wrong. I'm so sorry baby. Mommy is so sorry." My brother was trying to hold back his tears but they kept flowing. When my father put that belt to your backside, he makes certain to leave a memorable mark so that you won't make more bad decisions. My father made you not want to sit down after he finished whooping your behind.

My mother was in such disbelief. She appeared strong, but I knew deep down on the inside, she was hurting and wanted to break down, but she had to hold it all together for my brother. The expressions on her face showed that my mom was fearful of my father, but she kept it together for us. We never knew if our parents were going through anything because they never fought or argued in front of us.

The day had finally come, for me to get a whooping! It was my very first whooping. My father was very upset with me, I can tell by the disappointment he displayed on his face. I finally got in trouble and received that whooping I never

wanted to experience. The whooping

everyone else received except for me.

My day was here and I had no earthly

idea what was about to take place. I

carried on with my normal routine. I

thought I'd get away, but my father

had just about enough of my spoiled

ways. For some reason, I am mean,

always picking with everyone, but

never receiving any consequences for

my behavior. My grandmother,

mother, and father were all in the

kitchen, sitting at the kitchen table, I ran into the kitchen and stomped my grandmother's foot extremely hard with my hard bottom white shoes. My father didn't believe in whooping me, but this day I was in for a good old fashioned whooping by him. My father tore my butt up and that was the last whooping that I would ever get from him. My father looked at me and said, "Sandy baby, daddy didn't want to whoop your butt, but you know better than to stomp your grandmother's foot! Now go apologize to your grandmother right now, before I whoop you again." I hurried out of my father and mother bedroom, wiping my eyes as I continued to cry, trying to suck it up before I made it back to the kitchen where my grandma and mother sat. As I continued to cry, I went up to my grandmother and said, "Grandma, I'm sorry for stomping on your foot." My grandmother looked at me with her red, Indian skin tone, silky Indian wavy hair, and said, "Okay sweetheart, granny accepts your apology, but don't let that happen again okay? You know Grandma loves you!" I looked at my grandma and replied, "Yes ma'am Grandma. I love you too, while I wiped the tears from my eyes!"

Chapter Two

Evicted

As time passed, we enjoyed our family. We always have fun times with one another despite our dysfunctional family, forgetting about the past and focusing on the right now. After all, who had time to walk around moping everyday instead of enjoying family and life itself? I was on a natural high, putting the past behind, but beginning to aggravate my brother. I never bothered my sister because she stayed out of the way, but Major Lee, had a thing coming, because I was going to have fun terrorizing him day in and day out.

Since my sister liked to strike a pose all the time, she walked around the house catching moments of us on camera. If she wasn't behind the scene taking pictures of everyone, you could catch her posing at the drop of a camera flash. She had that natural pose. My sister was about 4'4", petite build, caramel smooth skin, with long black hair, and dark brown colored eyes. She wasn't an average girl. She is very intelligent, and beautiful. She is the girl everyone wanted to model after. She had her own style, she is one of a kind and she is my sister.

I liked to run back and forth down the long, beige carpet floored hallway, in and out of every room in the house. My brother always sat by our sister room so that he could roll his cars and trucks up and down the hallway.

Making sounds with his voice, vrrrrmm, vrrrrmm, while he rolled his cars and trucks into the hallway. At times, I ran pass him and kicked his pile of sport cars and army men, until they were all scattered throughout the hallway, and then I jumped over the hot flaming floor heater, only to land on the other side by our parent's room, laughing the entire time. He screamed at me, "Stop Sandy, I'm telling mom!" I'd run past him again, with an evil sniggle, while kicking the rest of his cars he had left, that was lined up.

It's still ironic that I had not seen anything strange going on between my father and mother. I don't think my brother and sister notice anything different between our parents either. I mean, they never mentioned anything to me about any unusual behavior they may have noticed. They didn't have any unusual marital issues. If they did, they surely did hide them without anyone noticing a problem.

Out of know where, something drastically happened amongst the family that my mother and father started arguing. My mother and father were in their room hollering loud. We stood by our parent's room door listening through the big thick sturdy brown wood door. I couldn't understand exactly what they were saying, but I knew it wasn't about something good. My mother was crying. My father and mother were arguing and this was serious. We knew not to knock on their door when it was closed, so we didn't bother. I heard her mention my sister Clovers' name. Clover looked at me in a disturbing way as she walked away down the hallway towards her room.

Clover didn't talk much. She stayed off to herself a lot. She didn't show her feelings, so that made it difficult to understand her and know what she could be thinking. She was very smart in school. She didn't have to study that often, because she is a student who can listen in class and Ace any test or pop quiz her teachers gave. She stood out from me and our brother. She stood out from her peers. She is different in her own way. She smiled a lot but though she showed no emotions she was hurting and no one understood her pain.

Back to the last time I recall living with my father. We were outside in the driveway with blankets, I was crying wondering what was going on, but my sister and brother acted as if nothing bothered them. My mother was picking up our belongings off the ground, as she made a phone call to her sister LuAnn. She was talking quietly, but nervously. She asked my Aunt if she could come and get us, while she continued to explain what had just happened between her and my father. I couldn't understand why my father had put us out, but we were out of the house. This had turned out to be a frightening and turbulent time. I am in total disbelief. I couldn't phantom the thought of daddy doing

us the way he did. As young as I am, I

knew that something wasn't right, but

didn't know exactly what it could be,

for daddy to make this all wrong. I

knew daddy as a provider, a protector,

and a God-fearing man who loved his

family. But daddy was humiliating the

family values. Daddy had made us

sleep outside on the concrete

driveway, with dirt and hard rocks.

How could this be? What was the

cause of him treating us like we were

stray dogs, that had just attacked him

and left bite marks in his skin, down

to the white meat? Who would have

known the cause of this situation

other than our mother and father?

Someone had to know something.

Somebody had to be behind this

traumatic family turmoil. I kept trying

to find the answers to all the questions

I had conjured in my small little brain.

I wanted to know why were we being

evicted from our home that we lived

in, and why was our father the one

doing the evicting? Questions raced

through my mind as I laid my head on

the blanket while I was forced to lie

on the concrete, in the driveway by

the gate.

Chapter Three

Separation

My mother and father separated when I was around three years old. I do not recall much of the moving process, but I do know we wasn't with daddy any more. I remember going to stay with my maternal grandmother for a while. My mother took us to Holly Springs Mississippi to visit with our grandmother until she could get things straightened out. We went back and forth to see our grandmother during the summer whenever my siblings were out on break from school. But during this time, when our father and mother split, we stayed the entire summer with our grandmother. We didn't spend much time with our father while we were at grandma house, but he did come by from time to time to bring us some money. Not seeing our daddy every day did not affect my siblings in any kind of way, but it kind of had a little effect on me. I knew that visiting grandma was a normal routine for us because grandma Almika wiped all our worries away. She knew how to smooth things over even when things seemed to be hard to cope with.

We returned back to our hometown, Memphis. Our mother had an apartment, a new place we could call our own. We were finally in our own home. I am ecstatic, but kind of sad because I am use to going home to my daddy. My brother and sister were extremely happy. I don't think they cared much for our father.

The transition of getting adapted to our new home, took a minute, but we eventually adjusted to coming home without our father being in the household. Lately I finally figured out that this is the way it is going to be since my parents are separated now. Our mother did not take us out of the school or church we were currently attended, she just couldn't see herself drawing any attention to the unforeseen circumstances my father had put her in. She is left to figure things out on her own with no help from my daddy, my mom stayed strong for us. Nothing really changed drastically in our lives other than our living arrangements.

My father had weekend visitation. He picked us up often and spent time with us, whenever my mother would allow us to go. Sometimes he picked us up from school on Friday's and took us back to our mother's house late Sunday evening, after church services, but that didn't last long. I wondered, why did my father stop coming to pick me up for a while and what happened to our family. "Why was it so divided?" I thought to myself. "When would my questions get answered," I wondered! My mother never spoke on what happened but she sure did talk against my father a lot. He is all kind of no good

motherfucker's.

After all, the transition of moving

to another place without my father,

was so hard, I could barely cope. The

transition seemed not to bother my

siblings at all. Clover and Major Lee

didn't take the moving process to

heart, they were happy as ever.

Maybe they knew more than I had

known, which, I couldn't figure out

why my father and mother separated.

Whatever the reason was, it was all

kept a secret. This secret could not be disclosed because it would damage the family values.

I was still that same little happy chubby, sandy head little girl, but moving from a place we lived and called home and not being with my father began to take a toll on me. I became very emotional and angry. I acted out doing things that was not normal. I always wanted my daddy because I was used to seeing him pull up in the driveway with his 1976

Black Cadillac, with the telephone

inside the car. No longer would I see

my father every day, and I didn't

understand why, and I knew I'd better

not question my parents about grown

folk business. I knew to stay in a

child's place or else I would receive a

whooping that would remind me of

why children are to stay in a child's

place. Hearing my mother speak so ill

about my father, saying, she can't

stand that dirty bastard, with his

cheating ass, no good son of a bitch,

didn't change my perception of who

my father is to me. The love for my

father did not change because my

mother felt differently.

Chapter Four

New Home

We finally started settling into the new apartment home. It was a nice, roomy, white three-bedroom, with two full size bathrooms'. It had a walk-in closet in the master bedroom, a kitchen with a bar, dining area, and a den, with a covered patio. The apartment complex we moved into were very spacious and the upkeep of the grounds were amazing. The buildings were tall, gray, cemented apartment complexes. What was stood out about the name of the apartment was their name, The Difference Apartments. They were different. Living in the Difference Apartments, wasn't going to be so bad, after all. Me and my family started to warm up to a peaceful place we would now call home.

I got super excited because my mom tried to duplicate the place we had moved from. She did a great job, even though we went from a house to some apartments, it was still our very own and spacious. The apartments are huge, but not as huge as our family house, daddy now lived in with his new family. There were two doors to the entrance of the apartment. One door led into the den area and the other door went to the kitchen area, the doors were diagonally across from one another. The den area is where the parties would soon be held. My mother had her own portable bar in the den. On the brown portable bar, you could find liquor like, Jack Daniel, Red Wine inside a crystal clear wine bottle, we drunk wine like that at church during communion, and some brown hardcore Whisky.

As we exit from the den we could walk into the area that is called, the dining room. The dining room had a patio with glass sliding doors, is where I kept my pink huffy bike. Our dining room was very special because my siblings and I often sat at the table to play board games and eat as a

family. We also prepared meals for

our mother when she had to work

overtime. She worked overtime so

that she could continue to provide the

necessities for us and buy us some of

the things we wanted. Across from the

dining area, is, a great bar and the

kitchen area. When we walked out the

kitchen and turn left it led us down

the hall and on the left side of the hall

was a full-size bathroom. On the right

side of the hall is one room that my

brother and I shared. We had bunk beds in our room. Next to me and Major Lee's room, is our big sister Clover's, room. Clover had a room all to herself because she is the oldest in the house. We took a few steps down the hallway and it led us into my mother's room. Her room is the biggest of all our rooms. My mother had a full-size bathroom, a vanity and a walk in closet. The floor plan in our apartment is very big and spacious but it could never take the place of our

big house, but it was our very own. It

beat sleeping outside on concrete and

bunking with other family members,

in different places.

Chapter Five
Pool Time

The apartment complex we lived in had two big pool areas. It seemed like everybody from the apartments and surrounding apartments was at the pool near the complex where we lived. You had to be a resident or have a guest pass to swim. My brother and I would go to the pool, quite often. I learned how to swim just a little bit by going to the pool a lot. My brother Major Lee had to learn by someone tossing him into the pool forcefully.

It was this one older guy by the name of Big Johnny. He would take all the younger children and throw us in the pool. If you didn't want to be thrown in the pool by Big Johnny, you'd better stay outside the pool area. My brother Major Lee was super scared of Big Johnny throwing him in the pool. He would stay outside the gated pool to keep from being thrown in, but that didn't stop Big Johnny.

Big Johnny had another plan. He

walked outside the pool area and

walked by my brother Major Lee, as

if he was leaving the pool area, only

to turn back around when my brother

wasn't paying attention, and when he

turned back around quickly he swiftly

grabbed my brother from the backside

and carried him inside the gated pool,

to throw him in. Major Lee was

terrified, crying, but that didn't stop

Big Johnny. Eventually, Major Lee

got used to being tossed into the pool that he started running inside the pool area and jumping into the pool before Big Johnny would ever have a chance to catch him again and throw him in.

The day we went to swim, if Big Johnny didn't throw us in, he would surely pick us up inside the pool and dunk us. He was very playful. One day Big Johnny almost drowned my brother and that's when the dunking and throwing people in the pool had ceased. My brother went home and told our mother. Of course, you know

she was overly protective of him. She

worked for the apartment complex, as

an apartment manager, so she had say

over many things that took place at

the apartments. The very next day we

went to the pool, our mom escorted us

so that she could confront Big Johnny

and let him know she meant business.

It wasn't hard for mom to know who

Big Johnny is because he was once

again chasing someone else around

the pool area catching them and

throwing them in. Major Lee said, there he is mommy, that's him right there. Our mom called him over and starred him dead in his face while she turned red and her eyes turned green. She said," you look ugh here; if you put your hands back on my son, there's going to be some trouble. Don't bring your ass back to this pool area dunking and throwing these children in. The sign clearly says, no dunking and running in the pool area." Then she walked off while telling Major Lee to come on. I

started noticing that Big Johnny didn't

come to the pool as much anymore

and if he was there, he didn't play

around like he's use to doing.

Chapter Six

Molestation

Our mother did the best she could to raise us. She worked day in and day out to keep a stable roof over our heads and provide the necessities. She sent us to the best of schools by paying for our education. As you recall earlier in the story, I'm the youngest and wasn't of age to attend school. My siblings were in school.

Since I couldn't attend school, and daycare wasn't an option, my mom had our cousin, Emily, watch me while she worked and while my sister and brother were at school.

At first, going next door sounded exciting and what I thought would be fun because I was going to be around family nearly all day, someone I knew as my cousin but called her my Aunt. The day came for me to start going next door to my cousin house, it was around six o'clock in the morning during the time my mom was leaving for work. I took my quilted blanket that my grandmother had handmade for me, and some food to eat for lunch. To be quite honest, the only thing that stuck out to me and what I recall about this whole going to my cousin house experience, is, the horrific mortifying experience I encountered for quite some time. This is when my journey in life started becoming disruptive.

I remember being with Emily who drank heavily. While I was next door during school hours, all I did was watched television along with being fondled, by my very own cousin Calvin, Emily's son. Cousin Emily kept me Monday thru Friday, while my mother worked and my siblings were away from home, at school.

I loved to wear my brown cowboy boots and stonewashed jeans with a lot of pockets. This is how I got my nick names, Boots and Pockets. My

Uncle Buddy, my mother's baby brother gave me those nick names. I wore those names, and I wore them proudly. You see, everyone in the family spoiled me. I answered to the names whenever my Uncle and anyone else would call me Boots and Pockets. A lot of time my Uncle Buddy would say "Pockets." I grinned from ear-to-ear just hearing how he said it with enthusiasm.

Every day, I had to ride with my cousin Emily. Every time she went to pick-up her son Calvin, from school, there I was in the backseat of her 1980 Brown Cadillac two-door car listening to her A-track radio as it played music by the blues singer Al Green. It was like she purposely picked her son up early from school just so he could taunt me by messing with me inappropriately. After we returned back to their house, immediately I knew what was expected of me. I was programmed to act as if I had to go use the lavatory.

This became a routine that eventually one day I really did have to pee. I was told by my cousin Calvin to go straight into the bathroom every day when we came in from picking him up from school. Don't make it obvious, Calvin said.

Calvin forced me into the bathroom. He was like this big giant in my life that made me crumble when he indicated what he wanted me to do. Calving bullied me into believing I had to do what he told me and I better not open my mouth to speak out against his wrongful acts towards me. I didn't know anything else to do but to follow his commands.

Each day he rubbed his right hand up and down my pants, playing with my innocent vagina, rubbing my clitoris on the outside of my pants, as he begun to unzip and unbutton my pants, only to creep his brown paper sack hands inside my stonewash jeans with pockets. Calvin rubbed the outside of my white butterfly panties,

back up towards my pot belly

stomach, pulled my panties slowly

down so that he could put his hands

on my clitoris and inserted his pointer

and middle finger inside my vagina

and begin fondling me. As I lie on the

white tile floor of their bathroom, the

entire time, my hazel eyes were

closed, scared to death, crying on the

inside for someone to help me, while

my cousin got away with molesting

me. He pulled his fingers out showing

me how wet they were with creamy white stuff on them. I didn't know what was happening, all I know is that I wanted it to stop, just go away. This cruel act that Calvin pulled happened to me on a day to day basis for almost eight months. My fourth birthday had just passed. It was about three months into school and my cousin was still getting away with enjoying himself by molesting me. I had to endure this horrific experience for quite some time.

I wanted to speak out against the wrongful things that someone did to me, but I couldn't. I was too afraid to speak out because I wasn't taught how to fight off an attacker who was older than I was. I was only taught to obey adults and my older cousins. I didn't know what to expect if I did speak out, so I just kept quiet, quiet as a mouse. I felt trapped, I felt closed-in, but I felt like screaming. I silently cried out for help while the signs were so vivid but my mother chose not to deal with the circumstances that surrounded her baby girl, me. My cousin Emily also chose to ignore what her son was putting me through. I was only three and a half years old during the time this molestation started. Innocent, sweet, caring and loving I am, but that was being stripped from me right before my very own eyes.

Chapter Seven

A Funny Feeling

Our mother bought us another dog and we named him Snow. Our dog was little, with shaggy hair, and he was a dingy white poodle, that wouldn't get much bigger than a Chihuahua. Snow is a house pet. We had him since the time we moved into the apartment unit. I started abusing the dog, a reenactment from what I was used to seeing and hearing. I would holler at him and hit him with newspaper for no apparent reason.

The poodle had this nasty stuff he would do to everyone's leg. I didn't know exactly why he did what he was doing until I overheard my siblings mention it. They knew obviously but I had the slightest idea until I put two and two together. I thought what he was doing was funny, so I laughed aloud every time I saw Snow try to hunch someone's leg or objects like my stuffed animals. I would throw one of my stuffed animals on the floor and watch Snow run and jump on it and put a hump in his back all while moving his hind legs. I sure didn't try to stop him, it was funny to me.

I couldn't explain why I started getting this funny feeling in my private area. I couldn't explain what was happening to me, I didn't know how to control it. It was like a thump, thump, thump, thump, and then a sensation that went away after a few seconds. What was happening to me? I didn't know and I didn't tell anyone what feeling I was having. I didn't know any other way of how I could get the word out of what had been happening to me. I was being molested weekly by my cousin. No one ever notice what was going on with me, at least that what it seemed like or was it that everyone was so busy with their daily lives or dealing with things they had gone through that they just didn't know how to recognize the signs to help me? Did they even notice the times I would just sit, watch, and laugh as our dog humped someone's leg or a teddy bear? These were the questions that wandered through my head. No one really paid that much attention to me, which made it evident that I was all alone and it seemed as if no one cared about how I was feeling and what was happening to me.

Chapter Eight
Secret Revealed

As time passed, one day I finally spoke out. I went to my mother and said, "Mommy, I have something to tell you!" My mommy acted as though she was in tuned to what I was about to say, but her long, peanut shaped head was turned in the opposite direction, watching television and dosing off to sleep. I nudged her, "Mommy, I have something that I really need to tell you!" My mother looked at me with her grayish green eyes, and said, "What is it Sandy? I'm trying to take a nap. What is it?" I said, "Mommy, Calvin has been touching me inappropriately, and I'm afraid. I don't want to go back over Aunt Emily house. Please don't send me back. He has been touching me every day." The response from my mom was like, she knew what was going on, but there was nothing she could do about it because she said to me,

"Oh Sandy, go on out of here, you
don't know what you're talking
about!" I was disappointed because
from her response she gave, my mom
didn't believe me or either if she did
there was just nothing she could do
about it because she had no one else
to watch me during the day while she
was at work, so she had no other
choice but to let me suffer. I was
terrified about telling my mom
because I was uncertain of what might

go down with my family, after I decided to spill the beans about what my cousin had been doing to me, for quite some time. But I had to tell my mother, because I trusted that she would protect me.

The very next day, I was back to my regular baby-sitter, which indicated to me, that, my mother did nothing about my situation and she didn't care what was happening to me. She did nothing to help save me from being molested. How could this be happening to me? Who was going to help me? Who was going to stand up against Calvin and his malicious acts towards me? HELP-HELP is what I was crying on the inside.

Calvin is a slick teenager and a smooth talker. He is a thirteen-year old sick minded boy, and had a reprobate mind. I experienced what could possibly be my very last encounter with him, but I didn't know at that moment until my mom came home and stated that she had found someone else to come and babysit me. At some point I couldn't understand why my mother would continue to send me back to the environment that I told her was making me uncomfortable. I just didn't get it!

One Thursday evening, Calvin forced me into the bathroom. This day was unlike any other day. This time it was extremely different, very different. I had to do something before it went any further. Calvin laid me on the hard, white tiled bathroom floor, unbuckled my pants, pulled

them halfway down, unbuckled his

pants got on top of me and tried to

penetrate me. He was grinding me

with his hard penis, trying to insert it

inside of me. Sliding up and down my

vagina, Calvin grabbed his hard penis,

trying his best to insert it inside of my

small child vagina. As he tried to

satisfy himself with his selfish

behavior, I laid there with my eyes

closed, in fear, hands trying to grip

the floor as I prayed that he would

stop. I cried on the inside wishing someone would save me from this heinous act as he tried to continue to satisfy his sexual desire, until out of nowhere, he felt something warm and wet. In his sick mind, he thought he had made me leak in a way that was pleasurable to him, but that wasn't the case. What he actually felt was my urine. Yes, I was so afraid, that I had peed on myself. I was so terrified that I couldn't hold it any longer so I used the restroom in the position he had me in, while he continued to lie on top of me. I was horrified!!! My butt, my back and the floor was soaking wet and so were my clothes. Calvin didn't care. Calvin had become comfortable with getting away with fondling me every day and nothing ever being done about it, that he didn't realize what had happened. He thought that since I probably never said anything, he could go even further by trying to penetrate me. He continued trying to penetrate me until I started crying and shivering while the stonewash pants and plain white little girl panties I had on, were at my feet. He pulled one of my pants legs over my left foot and kept the other side on.

I started crying and telling Calvin, "I need to get your mom to tell her!" Calvin said, "Tell her what?" Tell her what just happened to me, I said, in my shivering voice! Calvin looked at me in a threatening way and said, "Tell her what?" That I peed on myself, I quietly said to Calvin.

Calvin looked at me and said, "Let me go out first and you wait a minute before you come out, and when you do go tell my mother what happened, tell her you couldn't make it to the bathroom in time. You hear me, he said in a rebutted way." I continued to cry and pleaded for him to let me go tell his mom. Calvin tried hushing me but that didn't work because I was horrified. I was crying hysterically, but all the time I was too afraid to tell on Calvin. Something had to be done about this, it has gone too far. I needed and wanted a change of clothes. Calvin standing about 5"1", black afro hair style, paper sack skin tone, broad shoulders, walked out the bathroom as if nothing ever happened. He went into his room and quietly closed the door behind him.

I walked in his mother's room. She was lying there consumed in her alcohol and watching her favorite soap opera, "All My Children." She asked me, "Sandy what's wrong?

Why are you crying? Why are your clothes wet?" I tried telling her that Calvin had me in the bathroom touching me inappropriately, but I couldn't get it all out. She yelled for Calvin. Calvin, come here, she yelled! Calvin came out of his room. Ma'am, he responded! Why is Sandy wet? His mother asked him! Aunt Emily, I said in my cracked voice, as I wiped my face while tears continued to roll down my cheeks, Calvin has been touching me. Aunt Emily looked at

Calvin in a strange way. Calvin jumped right in and said, "She couldn't make it to the bathroom in time, so I tried helping her and that is how she wet her clothes by accident." Aunt Emily was so full of liquor that she wasn't listening to what I was trying to tell her. Aunt Emily didn't hear what I had said, she just believed what Calvin had said, that I couldn't make it to the bathroom in time, that is why I was crying and why my clothes were wet. Deep down inside, I believe that my Aunt knew what had been going on all the time, but she just chose to ignore the situation, as my mother did too. They didn't care and had no concern to stop what was going on. No one listened to me! No one tried to find out, why I was always crying and acting entirely different than my normal behavior.

Did my Aunt not listen because she had been abused by a family member, or maybe even someone close to the family, had molested her?

It seemed as if she didn't care what her son was putting me through this tragic experience. Why did this happen to me? What made my cousin do this to me? Was he taught this type of behavior? Did he witness someone doing it to someone else? Or had he also experienced someone messing with him during his childhood? What was going through his mind as he fondled me?

Of course, my Aunt was a drinker and she was consumed in her alcohol.

She loved to drink Coke & Crown everyday of the week, and smoke her Winston Lite 100. So why did my mother leave me with Aunt Emily, knowing that all she did was consume herself in her drinking? Did she have no other options? Was she so bitter from the divorce that she just didn't care about the wellbeing of her children? Why didn't she remove me from the environment? Why did she continue to allow this situation to carryon? Did my mother not care?

Did my mother not love me? Did my mother feel that she had to make a living for her children and self that she had no other choice but to ignore her four-year old daughter cries out for help? I had all kind of questions going through my mind.

Yes, my mother eventually pulled me from going next door to my Aunt's house, but she did not press any charges or investigate the situation any further. She never questioned me about what was

happening to me. She never
mentioned what happened to me, she
never uttered a word. I never heard
anyone speak on the situation. I felt
that my mother couldn't see pass her
own hurt and abuse that she didn't
realize the things that were happening
to me could trickle down from me to
one day my children. Those things
would soon tarnish my life. I didn't
understand why my cousin Calvin did
something like that to me and to hurt
me. Even though I was so young, I

understood every event that occurred in my life. I had an ole soul, as if I had been here before. The situation was never brought up again until later on in my life as a young adult. No one ever spoke on the incident, as if it never occurred. This situation will follow me everywhere I go, it wasn't going away. I would never forget the horrific situation. This is when my troubles had started. I became unaware of the behavioral problems I was having. It became worse as time

passed.

Chapter Nine
Drunken Behavior

I started noticing my mother do
things I had never seen her do before.
She started drinking excessively and
partying. Majority of the parties was
always held at our apartment. When
my mother threw parties, it would be
mostly family and close friends of the
family, sitting around drinking,
listening to the down-home blues,

playing cards, and dancing, having a merry good time. Our family from Alabama, Atlanta, Chicago, and Mississippi drove up to attend the parties that were on the weekend and holidays. The parties were live, music booming, and food on point. During the adult parties, all the children is told to go to the back rooms and don't come to the front, but I was hard headed and didn't follow those rules. Every now and again, I would sneak away from my cousins and I ran in the front room and struck a move in front of the adults, to put on a show. From that point on, I was the only child who would be allowed in the front room with the adults during the parties. My cousins liked to play around with one another, but my mind was so mature that I'd rather hang around the older crowd, rather than the children.

I loved the attention that I was getting. Could that attention had stemmed from the molestation that my cousin Calvin imposed on me as the little girl that I am? I felt like I had been ripped of my childhood, but I continued to take the path as a little girl with lost provision.

One day during a party, I ran to the front where the adults were. This was the day that I started singing the blues and dancing like a little girl with some soul inside of her body. From that day, whenever there were parties, the adults wanted me to come and steal the show. I owned the dance floor now, and every time they had a gathering at our house, it became my party. My mother had countless parties with our family. I was the center of attention. I liked to dance and hang with the adults. I remember my Aunt Katie, Aunt Emily, Uncle Henry and his wife Aunt Nina, Aunt Jo, Grandma B, Aunt LuAnn and her husband Uncle Dave, Uncle Buddy and his wife Aunt Spicey, being at almost every party my mother hosted. She invited her close, close friends, to the parties. The parties were live.

Nothing but good, clean fun, lots of talking and playing cards, that is until her and my Uncle Buddy got into it.

Sometimes Uncle Buddy would get filthy drunk to the point he would be staggering. When he got to this point it was something that triggered something inside of him and my mother that caused a scene. The two always argued for some odd reason. Once we had a party at Cousin Emily house across the hall, that the police were called. And what do you know it was my mom and Uncle fighting.

Uncle Buddy was in a wheel chair,

inebriated, that he couldn't get up.

Here comes trouble my mother started

calling him all kinds of son of a

bitch's. You, sad piece of shit, said

my mother. Fuck you, with your crazy

ass, Uncle Buddy said to my mother.

My mom went running to our house

and when she returned she came in

with full force. I'll show you whose

crazy, as she broke the broom across

his back. It was a lot of yelling and

curse words being blotted out. My uncle had to be wheeled away in his wheel chair.

The apartment security came and said they received a disturbance phone call coming from Apartment 112. They questioned what was going on but because my mom put in an application to become an apartment manager of the complex, they listened to her loud mouth and escorted my Uncle out Aunt Emily's apartment, where the altercation occurred. He was trying to explain that she caused

the commotion but they weren't

hearing him because they sided with

my mom.

Chapter Ten
Two Perverted Men

My mother is back in the dating zone. It didn't appear to me that my father had caused pain to my mother's heart, would stop her from seeing a lot of men. She was dating and it wasn't just one man she was seeing, she had several men. Could the pain my father inflicted on her or was my mother so scorn that it caused her to see many men at one time? Was she so bitter that she became vulnerable to the deception of the different men that appeared in her life? Maybe this was the only way she knew how to deal with her pain. Regardless of what she had perceived, my mother was showing signs of desperation.

My mother had several men that would come over at different times and days. It seemed as if the few men she was dating tried taking advantage of me in all kind of slick ways. They wanted me to sit in their lap, while they watched shows on television,

sitting in my mother's room in her

brown leather recliner chair. The days

her men came over, I acted like they

were my company, why not, they

were happy to see me. My mom

friend Jake came over quite

frequently. They had to be in a serious

relationship because he came over

more than the other guys she was

acquainted with.

For some odd reason, Jake loved

for me to sit in his lap. He would

come over right before my mother

walked through the door from a long,

hard day's work. When she came

home from work and Jake, with his

tall, lanky, jerry curl wearing self, had

already been there for several minutes

before my mother came in with a

great big smile on her face,

undressing from her work clothes.

She took a quick shower and put on

some comfortable clothes so that she

could go into the kitchen and prepare

a meal: steak with onions, homemade

salad, fried corn, and cornbread for Jake to eat. While she was in the kitchen preparing the meal, I was back and forth from her room to the room me and my brother shared. Yes, my mom cooked us a meal to but not before she fixed Jake a plate and told me to go take it to him.

As I approached Jake with his plate, he looked at me with his big bubble eyes and said, "Thank you baby!"

Jake patted his leg, indicating to me, to sit in his lap and eat with him. I was happy to do what was signaled for me to do, without any hesitation, because I didn't know any better. I looked at it as being innocent, but my mother's man, had other pathetic shit on his mind. I thought this was the norm and it was okay. I saw it as receiving attention from Jake, because after all, I am the baby of the family, and I am spoiled, thanks to my father. Jake had other intentions in mind, but he probably thought that my mother would blow him away with her forty-five pistol she had hidden in her room somewhere, had he not been discrete at how he played his cards right.

It was always the same two men who wanted me to sit in their lap when they were over to our home, Jake and Steve. They wanted me to sit in their lap. I often felt something hard coming from the men laps, but I was too young and naïve to know exactly what their intentions were, even though my cousin had damaged

my mind, I was more so numb to a lot

of the shit, that people were doing to

me. My little red hand could feel

something extremely hard while

climbing in their lap. Eventually one

day, I realized and noticed what was

happening, these two men was getting

a hard-on. I ignored it and kept sitting

in their lap, but I was hesitant & it

became uncomfortable to me, but I

still proceeded to doing what was

asked of me, because I was too afraid

to say anything to my mother and I didn't know what would happen to me had I told someone. In my mind, I felt no one would believe me even if I did say something, especially my mother. I kept silent and did what Jake and Steve continued to ask of me and signal for me to do, because I was always taught to obey adults. I felt it was only right to not go against what they asked, even though it was inappropriate. My own cousin had molested me, so this kind of behavior coming from me, wasn't unusual. I was seeking for help but had no one to rely on.

This time, I was still young and didn't have a voice. I was afraid of men. I was afraid of people in general. Whenever they told me to do something, I did exactly as I was told to do. I thought when my mom men wanted me to sit in their lap, that it was okay, because my cousin fondled me and nothing was ever done about it. My mom never uttered a word about me sitting in her men lap, in fact, she was grinning and probably thinking, that's so sweet, they're bonding. Bull crap, this wasn't a bond I wanted to happen, but the men were bonding alright, they were turned on by little old me. My mother never said it was inappropriate for me to sit in Jake and Steve's lap. When my mother's boyfriends continued to sit me in their lap, I thought no more of it. I did want to speak out, but again in my mind I felt that my voice wouldn't be heard, even if I did speak out about what was going on.

I felt lost in life. But overall I was a loving and a respectful child who wanted to enjoy being a little girl. I didn't want my childhood to be stripped from under me, but of all the events that had taken place, I was left with not much of a childhood. I always wanted to please everyone. I wanted everyone to be happy and satisfied. I did just about everything and anything to be perfect and be accepted by everyone. But it seems as

if everything I did went unwarranted.

Chapter Eleven

School Time

I finally reached the age to attend
school. I attended the school my
siblings were enrolled at. We attended
St. Joseph Catholic School. Our
mother signed us up to ride the school
bus. The school van would only come
and pick us up and transport us to
school and sometimes we would be
dropped off at home after school. The
reason the request for transportation

came about is because our mother had

to be at work at 5:30 in the morning.

The bus driver, Ms. Naomi, was a

healthy lady with two sons and two

daughters, Ishmael, Viola, Rasheed,

and Chloe, who also attended St.

Joseph Catholic School. The bus

driver Mrs. Naomi became a really

good friend to my mother. Mrs.

Naomi made sure we got on the bus

safely, and when she dropped us off at

home, she made sure we made it in

without any problems. She kept in

contact with my mother throughout the school year.

One sunny, cool morning, when Mrs. Naomi picked up her regular load of children, we were on our way to school and a car ran the stop light and hit the bus. BOOM, is the sound we heard when the bus collided with the car. Everyone screamed on the bus. The school van did a 360 and hit the curb and I flew into the back of the seat in front of me. We were all terrified. Me and the other bus riders were escorted off the bus by the paramedics and placed on the side of the curb at Winchester Rd and Elvis Presley Blvd. There were ambulance and fire trucks all over. My nose started bleeding because I was all shook-up. Everyone that was on the bus was alright, just a little sore from the impact. Since that day, I have been terrified of accidents and riding in vehicles with other people. Mrs. Naomi was a very strong, loving, caring mother, and bus driver. Her children also rode the bus. She

contacted every parent to inform them

that we were involved in an accident.

The other bus riders, parents arrived,

a short time later trying to console

their children. Our mother arrived, a

short time after the accident and she

ran toward us asking were we alright.

We were checked out by the

paramedics for observations but my

mother took us to our very own

Pediatrician Dr. Terrell just to make

sure we were okay just as we said, but

we were all shook up and a little sore from the impact. We had never been in an accident but this was our very first one and hopefully our last.

I enjoyed attending St. Joseph Catholic School. Sometimes I would have some problems with my peers not liking me. My kindergarten teacher was mean to me, but overall, it was okay. It was this one little girl named Janet that always picked on me. This girl bullied me almost every day. I went home telling my mother. I recall my mother saying to me, "you better stick up for yourself, if you come home one more time and tell me what someone else has done to you, I'm going to give you the worse whooping of your life." At this point, I took that advice, because I didn't want a whooping from my mother. Janet decided to pick on me again. I told Janet, "Stop, messing with me!" Janet had a pattern of bullying me and because nothing was ever done about it, she decided to ignore what I was commanding her to do and Janet continued to antagonize me. At this point, I had about enough of Janet and her bullying ways. I decided it was time to fight back. The voice of my mother played repeatedly in my head. I hauled off and slapped Janet so hard, she started crying. Janet was in total shock. Everyone that stood around, watched in disbelief, that this sandy hair, hazel eyed little girl had retaliated. Not Sandy, everyone murmured. I wasn't known to bother anyone, but when I stood up for

myself, this changed the game. Janet

went and told the Principal that I had

slapped her. I was called into the

office. I was questioned and told that I

would be reprimanded for my actions.

I tried explaining what had happened,

but the Principal didn't believe me

and really wasn't interested in what I

had to say. I was in deep trouble and

had to stay in the office until my

mother arrived to pick me and my

siblings up.

When my mother pulled up in that red fire-bird Trans-Am car, Major Lee and Clover ran to the car to explain to our mother what had happened to me. They told her I was in the office and the Principal wouldn't release me until she arrived, but she had to come into the office. My mother stepped out of her car with her flat black shoes and grey, work uniform on, as she stormed into the office. The look on her face, told everyone who she crossed paths with, that she was mad as hell. As my mother walked through the two sets of double doors to enter into the building, she went in ready to go completely off on anyone who stepped in her way. The Administration was already waiting for her, so when she walked into the office, they immediately escorted her into the Principal's office where I was sitting nervously, biting my finger nails, not knowing what the outcome would be because I slapped Janet so hard, until she turned firecracker red in the face. My mother started letting

the Principal have it. She spoke in a

heated tone telling Mrs. Susan, that I

was coming home every day saying

that this same little girl had been

bullying me and that I had told the

proper authority, but no one ever

handle the situation about how Janet

was constantly picking on me, every

day. My mother said, "I told her to

fight back. She has the right to defend

herself. And if anyone has anything to

say about what I told my child, then

you can see me in court, because I will have every single one of your jobs! If you mess with my daughter for defending herself, I'll take this to the Diocese and get a lawyer." My mother was furious! The Principal, my mother and Janet's mother, all had a conference concerning this incident. When my mother came out of the office, I didn't know what to expect from that day forward.

We were on our way home, my mom said, "Sandy, you don't have to worry about any other occurrences. I'm going to settle this once and for all!" She was fire hot. She was cursing like a sailor. She said, "I told that damn principal, if I have to go to the Diocese she isn't going to like it! Shit, damn it to hell! I'm not going to play with them. They allow someone to mess with you and when you defend yourself, it's a problem. I'll give their ass a problem. I will have her position and every teacher there, position. I'll be running that school or have that motherfucker shut down.

Shit!!!"

I understood that my mother took care of business and was not playing around, but was all that cursing necessary? I was kind of smiling knowing that my mother stood up for me. But on the other hand, I wasn't sure what to expect from my teacher when I returned to school tomorrow. Nervously as I pondered, I put my fingers in my mouth and started biting the little brittle thin nails that I had left.

My mother was so mad that she cursed all the way home. Those motherfuckers, sorry ass fuckers, don't know who the hell they are fucking with. I'll have every one of them son of a bitches, job. They better think twice about the shit they call themselves doing. But as soon as my child defends herself, now they decide to have a problem. Damn it to hell, she yelled!! I've told them they better

get their shit together.

My mother was furious about the

entire situation. She lit her Virginia

Slim cigarette after Virginia Slim

cigarette, as she drove home. She

flicked the cigarettes out of the car

window and lit another one. My

siblings & I sat quietly listening to her

rage about how the school had just

caused an up roar. My mother didn't

take any stuff from anyone. She is

that type of mother that if you stood

in her way, you were sure to get

cursed out.

Chapter Twelve
My Journal

My kindergarten teacher didn't
care much for me. Mrs. Lela had
locked me in the closet on several
occasions and made me stay there for
quite some time. My nose started
bleeding. Mrs. Lela wouldn't let me
come out of the closet to go to the
restroom so she sent one of my
classmates inside the closet to bring
me some Kleenex. I had a voice but I
didn't know how to use my voice to

speak up and speak out against the

heinous abuse the teacher was

showing towards me. I was so afraid

to say anything to anyone because I

was trained to keep my mouth closed

and don't say a word because if I did I

would be in trouble. The only way I

know how to deal with every

challenge I am faced with, is to let

people walk all over me, while I

continued being naïve and sweet to

them. I wasn't taught to speak up for

myself, so that is something I never did.

One day when my teacher put me in the closet, my older sister Clover witnessed it and became frantic. Clover would frequently check on us for some odd reason or another, but she made sure her siblings were taking care of. The day she became fed up with me being sent to the closet she was peeping through the classroom window and didn't see me sitting in the class, so at this time she knew I was in the closet. Later that day, I found out that someone knew that I was being mistreated was when we got home from school my sister told our mother what she had been noticing.

The next day we got up and dressed for school, our mother was still home. She said she was off because she needed to take care of some business. She took us to school, stormed into the school and gave Principal White and Mrs. Lela a mouth full. This would not be the last encounter I would be faced with during my time at St. Joseph School. I had a long journey ahead of me.

I started recording what I went through. I was gifted with writing poetry but I didn't know this, I just wrote. And because I was so close to my grandmother, my first poem I ever wrote was about her. It went like this: *Short, chubby, and as gentle as a drifting leaf, My Grandma sits and chats with me. It seems to me that every year she grows a little stronger,*

and it seems that every birthday, she

becomes a lot younger. Her

wonderful, witty personality makes

her a child just like me. I know this all

might sound quite odd, but my

Grandma is certainly a gift from God.

School became hard to deal with
because of all the commotion that was
going on around me. I just wanted to
make friends and have some good
friends that liked me as I liked them,
but unfortunately, I stood out for

some reason and that sadden me. My teacher didn't like me and I wasn't certain if it is because of me or if my mom's attitude and demanding crazy ways was the cause of no one being close to me. I really feel the teacher didn't like me because she had something against my mother.

As I prepared for bed, I started thinking about how my day would be at school tomorrow. I enjoyed school but since my mom couldn't hold her temper and she decided to curse everyone out, I was dreading going back to school the next day because I did not know what to expect from the Principal, Teacher, and my school mates.

Chapter Thirteen

Unknown Anger

The numbness I had built up
inside of me from the pain I felt from
my cousin molesting me started to
kick in. I didn't care about anything
anymore. Why did I have to care,
when no one cared how I was being
treated? Everything that had been
done to me became a rod of steel.
Nothing bothered me any longer. I

fought back by attacking others close to me. I started taking things out on my brother. Whatever was being done to me, I would pick fights with him to release the built-up anger I had inside of me. Little ole me bullied my big tall lanky brother. I didn't care that about him being a couple of years older than me, I felt that standing up for myself against Janet, gave me a boost of energy and a bit of confidence to go up against anybody, so I chose my brother to pick on. This was different from sibling rivalry, this

was revenge coming from an angry,

messed up, abused, innocent little girl

who was stripped of her childhood

and had to start living a pretend tough

life. The abuse that I endured made

me act out looking for attention and

an escape out of the hell that was in

my pathway.

My brother is a momma's boy

so that gave me even more reasons to

pick fights with him. She paid more

attention to him than she did me and

my sister Clover. Since he wanted to be a momma's boy, so he can run and tell her that I am picking on him, with his scary butt.

One day we were sitting around and I got bored so I ran in the kitchen and pull out the biggest butcher knife we had in the house and chased my brother around the house. He took off running like the cartoon character, the roadrunner, and started yelling, but the only other person at home is our sister and she really didn't watch us.

At no time, did she feel like being bothered with us, so whatever my brother and I did, she ignored us, just as long as we didn't hurt one another.

I laughed and laughed as my brother ran throughout the house trying to escape. Major Lee ran into the hall bathroom where he locked himself until someone came to rescue him. He was terrified and didn't know exactly what I was going to do with the big, black handle butcher knife. I knocked on the bathroom door yelling, "Come on out Major, so I can kill you! I'm tired of you messing with me. Come on out!" Our sister came out of her room and looked at me. She said, "Telephone! Momma wants to speak to you."

Hello, as I put her blue rotary phone to my ear. "Sandy, I'm going to beat your ass when I get home. Put that damn knife up, my mother said. What the hell is wrong with you? Why are you acting like a heathen?" But momma, as I tried to explain!

Major has been messing with me and I'm tired of him. I don't care what he is doing, that doesn't give you a reason to grab a knife and chase him with him. You just wait until I get home, you won't pick up another damn knife in my house. Shit, she said, as she hung up the phone.

Saved by momma as usual, Major bony, big teeth butt would've been cut real deep had momma not said anything. I'm sick of him laughing and messing with me. I really enjoy taking control of the situation and feeling like super woman with power as I chased him throughout the house with a knife. Little ole me finally found something that would make him run like a bitch.

My brother had company. His best friend Butch was over our house to visit. No one knew about the crush I have on Butch. I am feeling him, especially with his brown smooth skin tone, standing about 5'4", big eyes that I catch staring at me sometimes, but Butch Oh my goodness is as cute as can be, just the type of boy I liked. I wanted Butch to notice me, and when I heard them talking about girls and I wasn't the topic of his conversation, I decided to break that conversation up. They were having boy talk alright, talking about girls and planning to go to a dance and talking about what they are going to wear and who they were after, is just what I needed to create a scene and bring their talking to an end.

I walked in the front room where they were sitting and planning, then all I hear is my brother say, "GET OUT OF HERE SANDY!!!" I was furious, so I stormed into the kitchen, opened the kitchen drawer where the knives were, grabbed a knife, and ran out the kitchen charging at my brother. Before I could make it to him, they had knocked over the kitchen chairs trying to run because Major Lee had already yelled to Butch, she got a knife, RUN! I chased both of them with the long, sharp, black butcher knife that I had in my right hand. They ran and locked themselves in the hall bathroom until I chose to give up and go put the knife back in the kitchen drawer.

I was so spoiled, that it made me already being mean, rough, tough, and bad even worse because of the molestation I had went through. I don't think I was aware of how much my behavior had changed, but I knew I had become extremely active and got into a lot of things that would

cause me to get in trouble. By the

time I was promoted into the second

grade, I was terrible. My behavior

became extreme.

Chapter Fourteen

The Day I've Waited For

My brother liked to play with his trucks. He had tons of trucks in his possession. On some days, I wanted to play with him but he was so mean to me, he wouldn't let me join in his playtime. My brother would pull our dog around on his big black steel Tonka truck. As days went by, I continued to bother my brother, that made him give up and decided that it would be best if he let me play with him. Major Lee thought it would be a great idea to pull me on the same big black Tonka truck that he pulled our dog on. This was my brother's brilliant idea to get back at me for bullying him in my own little small way. He tortured me from all the mean things that I had been doing to him. This was surely payback! Major Lee pulled me on his truck so fast that he made me fall off. All because I was rough and tough, I found this to be amusing. I laughed until my stomach started hurting. I turned red in the face from laughing so hard. I enjoyed riding on my brother's truck, but one thing I didn't realize is that he was trying to hurt me. He thought it was funny but he also had something else in mind. He was trying to hurt his baby sister in a way that look like fun but could cause a great deal of pain. My brother didn't have good intention for me being on his truck because he felt that I was annoying all those times he was playing by himself and he told me to leave him alone, but I wouldn't. We begin to fight all the time because we were so close in age, but mainly because I had gone through a lot in my first few years of life, that I had to find somebody close to me to take my pain out on. No one could understand why I had become so mean and always pulled knives out to harm my brother, all they knew was that I changed, and it wasn't for the good.

My sister Clover was always quiet. She stayed to herself and didn't like to be bothered. She stayed out of the way of me and our brother. She didn't want any dealings with our sibling rivalry.

My mother worked long hours. She allowed me and my siblings to stay at home alone. Sometimes we went to work with her when she had to do overtime. The times we stayed at home, our cousin Emily, who still lived next door to us, would check on us periodically. My sister was old enough to keep us until our mother could find another sitter, but our mother was taking precautionary measures just in case something happened, she had back up to keep an eye on us.

My Aunt LuAnn, my mother's sister, gave a name of a young lady who lived down the street from her. We met Ms. Dobb. She took the offer that was presented to her and begin keeping us. Ms. Dobb had two sisters.

Her sister Sheryl was a sitter for my
Aunt LuAnn, her other sister Draya
was the same age as me and she
would sometimes come over when her
sister came to sit with us.

Ms. Dobb would come on certain
days to babysit. While Ms. Dobb was
in the den area, my brother, Draya and
I were in the room playing. My
brother and Draya would gang up on
me and tell me to sit inside a big
brown box. They closed me inside the
box and would not let me out. After

211

numerous attempts of trying to exit

the box, I became frustrated, hot, and

started crying because I couldn't

breathe. My brother and Draya

laughed and continued keeping me

closed inside the box. Finally, Ms.

Dobb came to check to see what was

going on and that is when she found

out what Major Lee and Draya was

doing to me. Ms. Dobb let me out and

then she took the box because she

knew that Major and Draya were

going to try and lock me in the box

again. I leave y'all to play and be good but here it is y'all are causing this child to have an asthma attack, said Ms. Dobb.

We found something else to do because the box was taken away from us. Next, my brother came up with the idea to take my slide and put it on the bunk bed so that we could slide down and off the bed. I wanted to participate but I didn't want Draya getting on my slide because she was too big and could possibly break it.

We started arguing about this, and I think that argument led to Draya not coming over anymore when her sister would come to babysit. I really didn't care because I didn't want her fat ass breaking all my toys.

I am very protective of my toys, unlike my mother not protecting me from letting horrible shit happen to me. I didn't want my toys broken, plus I had been through so much that it made me extremely mean towards people. This caused me to not get along with people, but it wasn't because I didn't want to, I just didn't know how to treat others when I had been treated so horrible myself, by the people I thought loved me. I overreacted on everything. I couldn't help my thought process, and at the time, I didn't understand what was going on with me. I just know that the things happening to me wasn't right and it sure didn't feel right.

Our mother picked up a second job to make ends meet. She worked at the apartment complex where we lived. This required for Ms. Dobb to come over more often than her usual days. As my mother worked, Ms. Dobb came over on the days my mother had to work overtime. The babysitter only worked for a few months until my mother could equip us on how to stay at home alone and until she felt we had it mastered and were safe.

Chapter Fifteen

Accident Prone

I became rebellious at an early age. My mom was barely at home, always working or working late. We had to cook for ourselves. My brother Major Lee was the one who had learned how to prepare breakfast and fry some bologna, and Clover learned from her Easy Bake Oven how to cook a few things. There were times when my siblings and I thought that our mother would be home at a

certain time, so we prepared a surprise

meal for her. While my brother and

sister cooked the meal, I set the table.

We cooked and lit candles to surprise

her. We hid under the table so long,

that we fell asleep under the table

waiting for her to walk through the

door. But we stayed in the dining

room because we could wake up

quickly when we heard her put the

key in the door to unlock it. Finally,

we heard the sound of the door being

unlocked. Momma walked through

the door and we jumped up and said,

"SURPRISE!!" She didn't appear to

be surprised at all. She said, how nice.

But by this time, the food was cold,

and she was too exhausted to eat what

we had prepared for her. She told us

to put it in the refrigerator and she

would warm it up later. We were sad

because every time we tried surprising

her, she was always too tired to enjoy

a meal we went out of our way, to

prepare for her because we know that she worked hard every day.

One day my brother Major Lee was in the kitchen fixing him some breakfast. I wanted something to eat too. My brother didn't want to fix me anything to eat, so I pulled my high chair up to the stove and sat patiently waiting for him to finish cooking. Major turned the stove top off and started laughing. I retrieved one piece of sausage patty from the package. I patted it together, and threw it in the skillet, while it was still sizzling hot.

The sausage landed in the skillet and I

quickly drew back my arm as the

sausage patty started frying and the

grease started popping. My small,

narrow elbow hit the handle of the

skillet, turning it over. The hot

sizzling grease dropped onto my left

leg, burning me intensely. My foot

covered red pajamas were stuck to my

leg. Major put his food down and

tried helping me out of my high chair,

rushed me into the hall bathroom,

closed the door, and said, "If you don't tell momma, I'll fix you something to eat!" Major tried running water on my leg to remove the pajamas but they wouldn't bulge. Leaving no little to no friction at all to remove the pajamas away from my body. The pajamas were now stuck to my left leg, giving me and my brother no other choice but to run and tell our mother what had just happened. I rushed to get our mother, while Major was too afraid of what might occur from the horrific incident that

happened because he was being mean

to me and wouldn't cook me any

breakfast. Major Lee lagged behind

me not wanting to approach our

mother's bedroom where she was

sound asleep. She didn't like for us to

disturb her while she took a nap, but

we had to let her know what just

happened. I started speaking with my

little sweet voice, afraid to bother her

as I called out, "Mommy, mommy".

She didn't hear me. I called out again,

only to move closer to nudge her as I called out to her, "Mommy, mommy", I called! My mother jumped up in a panic, "what is it?" I pointed at my leg as I tried to explain what happened. My mother looked at the place I was pointing at and asked, "What happened, hysterically?" Major started stuttering as he tried to explain. I was in the kitchen cooking me some breakfast…" I interrupted, "I wanted some breakfast but he wouldn't fix me any, so I threw a piece of sausage in the skillet, and my elbow hit the handle, causing the hot grease to waste on me." My mother pulled out her first aid kit while she tried to remove the pajamas from my body. She realized that the pajamas were not coming off easily. She knew this was serious, but she didn't panic because she had at some point been in the medical field. She pursued nursing as her career, but didn't finish because of the separation from my father.

I had a serious burn that needed medical attention. My mother knew that she would have to rush me to the hospital. They packed up to leave the house. Got in the two-door red Trans Am that their mother drove. She idled up her engine, put the pedal to the metal and took off in her Firebird Trans Am. Momma didn't do the speed limit on the way to the children's hospital. Upon arriving at the hospital, she parked her beaming red Trans Am in the parking lot of the hospital. Got out the car carrying me to the front entrance, my mother sat me inside of a wheelchair. We went through the double doors of the hospital and checked-in. They immediately rushed me to the back to and checked my vital signs. The nurse asked me, "Are you in any type of pain?" I responded, "No ma'am. It's just stinging a little bit." They had to cut my red pajamas off my leg to see the site of the burn. When they examined the site, they determined they would have to do emergency surgery because the burn was serious. I had second degree burn. My thigh was red, swollen with blisters all around. The burn covered the entire left thigh. After determining that my burn was serious and required surgery, they began prepping me for surgery and gave me some sleepy gas. The last thing I recall before drifting into lala land; was the doctor asking me, "Are you getting sleepy yet?"

Before you knew it, I was out for the count.

When I awakened, I was still in the hospital bed with machines hooked to me, and a big bandage on my left upper thigh. Surgery was over just that fast. I looked around to see my mother in the recovery room with me. I sat up and asked, "How long have I been sleep?" She responded, "Oh Sandy, only for about forty-five minutes!" I said, "It seems like I've been sleep for hours." Yes, I know

Sandy. That's how the medicine makes you feel, and that is the best sleep ever, my mother said."

I am a strong little girl. I quickly recovered from the burn to my leg. It was as if, nothing ever happened to me. I took that burn to my upper thigh and didn't let that stop me from being active and doing the things I liked to do. At some point, I started doing too much. One day, the burn on my leg started getting infected. I had to return to the hospital for further observation.

My mother took good care of the burn
and she used her expertise on what
she knew to do. She had to change the
gauze constantly and apply betadine
and antibiotic ointment to the burn
more than twice a day. After a long
journey, the burn healed but there will
always be a scar on my leg that will
remind me of the hot grease that fell
on my thigh.

For a while, my brother was very
careful around me, but he made little
slick comments about my burn, like

"That's what you get! That's why you got burned!" I didn't care what he said! I continued being the active little girl I was known to be before the incident occurred. The burn didn't stop me from being overly active. Since my brother didn't get chastised for the burn he caused, he felt he could be mean to me and nick pick.

Chapter Sixteen

Acting Out of Resentment

By the age of six, I had
experienced a lot in my short life
span. I was always signaled out by
teachers, peers, and even my own
mother. My brother Major Lee would
even tease me for no apparent reason.
I started feeling like he hated me. I
became rebellious and disobedient.
Things had begun to happen to me on
a constant basis. I got into a lot of
things that would draw attention to

my life. I was seeking for love because my mother seemed not to love me, and now my brother was also acting as if he didn't love me. My sister Clover always kept to herself, that I didn't bother her too much. She liked to be left alone.

One day, my family & I were in the house taking a nap. At least everyone else was taking a nap, but me, No, I had to be disobedient and stay awake to get into something else. I heard a knock on the door and went to the door. I noticed it was my friend Raven. Raven asked me, "Can you come outside to play? It's a fire in the apartments across from us!" I told Raven, "yes, just a moment." Raven told me to give her my bike so she can ride it! I knew I should've been taking a nap and not out of the house, but going outside sound more like fun than taking a nap. I snuck out the house anyway, but before going out the den door, I passed Raven my pink huffy bike, over the balcony. Raven got on my bike and started to ride off.

I ran behind her just a giggling away,

not knowing that I was destined for

trouble. Here I go running behind

Raven following her to the apartment

fire.

When I made it to the back of the

apartments where we lived, I saw a

bunch of fire trucks and people

standing afar off. The apartments that

had caught fire, was another set that

was directly across from the

apartment complex we tenants in.

Someone called out my name. Sandy, they yelled! I turned around to see who was calling my name and little did I know it was my cousin Calvin. You know Calvin, the one who molested me when I was three and four years old. Calvin was sitting on the log fences watching the blaze as fire fighters tried putting out the fire. Calvin said to me, "You shouldn't be out of the house. I'm going to beat you home and tell your momma." I looked at Calvin and said, "No! You won't beat me, I'll beat you." I took

off running back towards home,

leaving my bike behind. I was

determined to beat Calvin back

toward the house, so that I could go in

the house and play sleep. That was the

plan I had running across my mind. I

took the only way I thought was the

quickest way back home. This was the

route I traveled from time to time,

throughout the Apartment complex,

whenever I was allowed to play

outside for a while. There were

several ways to get to certain parts of

the apartment, and this was the fastest

way I knew to detour through the

back of the apartments. At least I

thought it was the quickest way back

to the apartment units where we lived.

As I was running home, I kept

looking back thinking Calvin would

be behind me, but he was nowhere in

sight. I was running fast as I could. I

was dodging in and out of the

individual apartment complexes. As I

approached a curve about twenty-five

feet from the front door of our apartment, I met up with a neighbor riding his ten-speed bike. I was running so fast trying my best to beat Calvin to my house, that I didn't realize it was a boy on a bike coming around that same curve going but coming in my direction. I turned around from looking back and boom! I collided with Jason on his bike. My nose hit the rim of the tire on the bike and I flew backwards into the corner of a log.

I had one thing on my mind. I couldn't stop there. I had to beat Calvin to the house. I got up from off the ground, looked at the boy, felt something running from my nose, put my hand on my nose, only to wipe and saw blood on my hand. The boy picked up his bike and looked at me with a scared look on his face. I told him, don't worry about it and I started back running toward home. As I was running, blood was running from my nose leaving a trail behind me. I held my nose as I continued to look back to see if Calvin had caught up with me. When I ran those few extra steps to the front door of our apartments, Calvin was already standing at the door. I ran past Calvin, bust through the door, into the house I went, to awake my mother. My mother got up in a panic to find blood gushing everywhere. My nose was bleeding tremendously. When my mother realized that she couldn't get the blood to stop with pressure applied to my nose, she gave me a cold towel

and said, "Your nose is broken, I have

to take you to the hospital." I looked

in the mirror and saw clear as day that

my nose is out of place. It is sitting

under my left eye, twisted, still

bleeding. My mother told my sister

and brother to get dress so that she

could rush me to the hospital.

We got in the red two-door

firebird car. My older sister Clover sat

in the front passenger seat while I sat

on the arm rest in the middle of the

driver and passenger seats. Major was in the back seat. Clover and Major were crying, but I was laughing. Blood was gushing everywhere. It was certain that I had a broken nose. I had to undergo emergency surgery. They placed metal pins in my nose. The pins will stay in my nose permanently. All I remember is when the doctor put the mask over my face and I snatched it off when I felt myself drifting off to sleep. They told me, "Sandy, you have to keep this on your face, so that you can rest." They placed the mask back on my face, and told me to count to ten. I started counting, 1-2-3, and out I went. I was out like a light, no remembrance of anything occurring after I got to 3.

After I awaken, I was surrounded by the doctors looking at me. I don't remember anything about the surgery. But I do remember being sleep for what seemed to be hours. There were all kind of monitors hooked to me, to stabilize my vitals. The doctors monitored me for a few hours before

releasing me to go home.

Chapter Seventeen
Confession of My Sins

I was promoted to the second grade and I have reached the grade level to receive first communion. This was my mother's decision. In the Catholic Religion, a child is only allowed to receive first communion when they reach a certain age. First Communion is when a child can receive the body and blood of Jesus Christ. They call this accepting Jesus as Lord and Savior in a Catholic Church. Many of the other girls and I, wore a white dress and a veil that covered our faces, on one evening while participating in Mass. This type of Mass is held for children who will receive their very first communion and confess Jesus as Lord. This commitment would also acknowledge that if we sinned we would have to confess our sins before the Priest of the church, who is supposed to pray for us and forgive us of our sin. It is a tradition for the family, that whatever your mother's religion is, the children had to be of that same religion. Whenever I would go before the priest to confess my sins, it went a little something like this:

Priest: *What have you done that brought you here today?* **Sandy:** *I come to confess that I stole a pencil.*

Priest: *What were you thinking when you committed this sin?* **Sandy:** *I don't know but I won't do it again.*

Priest: *Your sins are forgiven. Let's*

us pray the "Hail Mary." Hail Mary,

full of grace, the Lord is with thee:

blessed art thou among women, and

blessed is the fruit of thy womb, Jesus.

Holy Mary, Mother of God, pray for

us sinners, now and at the hour of our

death. Amen!

This is how the confession session

would go every time you had a

confession to make. The Priest would

be behind a wall that blocked your

face from being shown to the Priest. I

had no recognition on why this had to

take place but I did it in accordance to obeying what I was taught about religion.

I had gone through a tremendous amount of terrible circumstances before age seven. I developed a relationship with a girl name Eva. Eva and I became the best of friends. Eva and I started getting into a lot of trouble together. Eva was a bad influence but we had fun together. We had another friend who would do some crazy things with us but she never got caught. Adrienne is a petite, paper sack, classmate, with long black hair. She was quiet but O so sneaky. She smiled all the time showing her pearly whites. Her facial expression is what fooled our teacher and what helped her stay out of trouble. See, Eva and I had that guilty face, and plus, Eva didn't make it any better, she would laugh when were accused of doing something we should have had sense enough to reverse the accusations, but no, Eva liked getting in trouble. One day Eva and I got in some major trouble at school that we lost our privilege to go to a class outing and we also had to stay after school to do some work for our punishment. I had written curse words on the back of one of my test paper listening to Eva and I had the nerve to turn it in to my teacher, Mrs. Walker. My mother came to the school without prior knowledge of what had taken place. She had some new shoes for me. But when my mother entered the classroom, the new shoes became a nonfactor because Mrs. Walker had already called my mother and informed her of what I had done. My mother was very upset, or could it had been that she was more so embarrassed at my behavior because it would reveal how foul her mouth is, or was she really that disappointed at me? After finding out what I had done, my mother had a rude awakening for me, but I was unaware as to what was in store. My mother asked me in front of Mrs. Walker, "Where are you getting these curse words from?" My mom didn't expect me to say, "I got them from you!" My mother turned pale with this stunned look on her face and then she became furious and asked the teacher to excuse her as she snatched me out of the classroom and escorted me to the restroom where I was about to feel the wrath of her anger. Eva sat back in her desk, trying to put on this persona as if she was innocent. She raised her big pop eyes up towards my direction, sniggled, as she continued writing.

My mother is a big curser but she didn't want to believe that I would pick those words up from her and use them and then blame her for why I was using those words. What was she to expect, when all she did was used profanity in every sentence she formed. Every other word was a curse word parting from my mother's mouth.

After she finished letting me have it in the restroom, she then turned to me and says, "This is the thanks you show me for buying you some new shoes?" No ma'am, I replied as tears streamed down my face. I was more hurt at her for being upset at me because she was the reason I started repeating curse words, more so than I was for her giving me a whooping for writing curse words down. But after she finished chastising me, she said, "I don't ever want to hear you do anything like that again. You hear me?" Yes ma'am! is how I responded in a shivering voice as I blew my nose from the snot running because I was crying.

We walked out of the restroom back to the classroom where Eva and I was serving after school detention for our behavior, and my mother made me apologize to Mrs. Walker for my actions. "I apologize, Mrs. Walker, for writing profanity on the back of my test paper. It won't happen again." Mrs. Walker had this look on her face like she had got me in serious trouble. As she looked at me she says, "I accept your apology Sandy, but I am expected better from you than that. You don't have to follow after anyone. It will get you in trouble in the long run." I knew Mrs. Walker only said that because she wanted so much to believe that I was copying Eva, when the truth was told that I got it from my mom, as I told them earlier.

Chapter Eighteen

Break-In

I was rough and tough. I loved to be outside playing. I loved to swim, and I loved to ride my bike with my friends. I was so rough, I often, like twice a week, bust the tires on my pink huffy bike. My father Major Jr. was tired of replacing the inner-tube in my bike every week, that one day he decided to try something different. One day, when my father brought my

bike back, my tires were different.
They were extremely different. I had
concrete tires. I was excited at first
because it was something that I never
seen before, but leave it to my father,
he knew all the tricks and trades of
solving a problem, in his own way. I
tried riding my bike for two weeks.
As I rode my bike, I became more
frustrated at what my father had done.
I told my father that it was a challenge
to ride my bike and I no longer
wanted those tires. My father told me,

"Well baby, daddy sorry, but you will have to deal with this for a while, because you keep running over things and busting your tires. Now you won't be able to bust these." I took that and went on to adapt to the concrete tires. I rode over everything, from glass bottle, to nails, to the potholes in the streets. It wasn't a limit to what I could run over. It even felt like I was going to bust up the concrete that I was riding on, with my tires. That's how hard they really are.

I definitely couldn't bust these tires. I liked to pop my wheels in the air, but having concrete tires, it was very difficult to perform this trick. I tried it anyway and became frustrated with the fact that the tires were so heavy I could barely lift the tires in the air.

One day, we came home and found that someone had kicked in our apartment door. Our dog Kesh, was hiding behind the brown bar that we had in our house by the front room window. This is the area in the apartment where the parties were held. Kesh was frightened, shaking and had feces everywhere. That same day, our mother, begin the preparation to move them from the Difference Apartments and searched for another place to live. Because our mother worked for the apartment complex, one day the maintenance men found some of our belongings in another vacant apartment unit. Our mother sent us to stay with our grandmother for the summer until she could maneuver and find another place to live. When we returned from out-of-town, my family and I had to live with Uncle Jake until our mother could find us a place of our own.

Uncle Jake lived in the only blue house on Woodbury St, in Memphis, Tennessee. Living with our Uncle was okay. It wasn't such a bad experience. At least we had a place to sleep and wasn't out on the streets. I can't recall staying with our Uncle for too long, but during the stay, we had fun as a family. I remember this as being the only time, in a long time our mother would really spend any time with us. We would lie around at night and watched scary movies, whenever our mother didn't have to work overtime on her job. She no longer worked for the apartment complex, but she still worked her job she had been on for five years.

The movies we watched were so terrifying that I couldn't sleep at night. I'm so terrified of scary movies and anything creepy. Uncle Jake was a fun uncle to be around. He would go outside and play with us. I rode my bike and yes, my daddy finally put regular tires back on my bike. We washed Uncle Jake's truck every weekend it was nice outside. He would take us to the corner store in his blue pickup truck and buy us candy and ice cream. Uncle Jake loved to have us around because he was lonely. He was no longer with his wife. He had been divorce for quite some time.

Time would soon come for us to move from Uncle Jake home. We aren't for sure when we were moving, but we knew it was close. Uncle Jake really didn't want us to leave, but he wanted his space back to himself. We promised Uncle Jake that we would come back to visit him.

Chapter Nineteen
Grandma's House

During the summer months, me and my siblings would go and stay with our grandmother in Holly Springs, Mississippi. My grandmother lived about an hour away from Tennessee. Almost everyone in the Mississippi is some kin to us, let my grandmother tell it. I loved going to spend the summer with my grandmother. Visiting Grandma

Annie was fun, entertaining, a getaway, and of course, those home cooked meals grandma made, are the bomb. Grandma Annie would cook the good old home country meals. My favorite meal of all times is the one when grandma would cook mackerel and rice for breakfast. I sopped up the syrup with the homemade biscuits grandma made. Mmmm, Mmmm good! My, my, my! This is some good old country eating, I thought to myself!

The hardest part about visiting grandma was when I had to get my hair comb by my big cousin Denise. She had to comb my hair on relentless times. I don't understand why she was stuck with that task instead of my big sister Clover. My hair is extremely sandy red and course. My cousin seemed to have a hard time combing my hair. I really think she didn't want to do it, but out of respect for her Aunt Asiana, she did what she was told to do. As Denise combed my hair, she was pulling and tugging on my head and mumbling. Of course, I don't want to sit still, because sitting on the hard floor with my head being pulled backwards and forwards, just wasn't an easy thing for me. Denise, I yelled! Shut up Sandy, she said! Sit here and get your hair comb! I don't know why I am always the one to comb your hair, when you have a sister. Every time we come to grandma house, I'm always the one having to comb your hair. "I don't know either, I replied. But you are hurting my head and I am ready to go outside and play."

At grandma house, we have too much fun. Me, my siblings, and my cousins, are always at Grandma Almika house. I loved to go outside and play in this concrete tunnel the apartments have throughout the property. My cousin and I would meet some of the young boys from the apartments that we had a crush on. Sometimes our cousin Dexter would go with us. And when he came along,

we had to be cautious as to what we

said at the concrete circle, made like a

tunnel. Everyone loved the concrete

tunnel. We would sit, stand, run

through, and jump off the concrete

tunnel. There wasn't very much to do

in the country but we found things to

do. We were a close nit family with

little to do, because we always found

a way to entertain one another. When

we had absolutely nothing else to do,

Grandma Almika would let us walk

across the busy intersection and go to the skating rink. The Ranking Circle Skating Rink was only open on the weekend, but we made the best of it. Everyone in Holly Springs came to the Rink. It was overly exciting because we were from Tennessee and Huntsville. We are like new faces in the town every time we visited.

My cousin Viola and I were two of the three youngest of the family, so we are the last to always be at Grandma's house without it being a holiday or special occasion. The grandchildren are so busy being teenagers and doing other things that the only time they would come to Grandma's house, is when we had Grandma's birthday parties, family gatherings, and our parents class reunions.

Let's go walking Viola! Sure, why not, she asked? We walked in the scorching heat, towards Rust College. Grandma Almika sent us her errand runs. We had to go across the street to the neighborhood grocery Piggly Wiggly to pay some of her bills. We walked to KFC to get food whenever grandma had a taste for the original chicken and whenever had to depend on others to do things for her. I told my cousin, every time we visit grandma during the summer months; it is always scorching hot as if God has a curse on Ranking Circle! It is just too hot here in The Sip! Whenever grandma didn't have enough ingredients for supper, she would send us to the store with a little

extra change to get us some chewing

gum or anything we'd want for going.

Grandma also did not have room in

her apartment for a washer and dryer,

so at times we would have to walk to

the apartment laundry mat to do the

dirty laundry. Most of the times

grandma washed her undergarments

out on her hands and hung them to

dry over the shower rod in her

bathroom. Visiting grandma is the

best, because we got to see family that

we wouldn't normally see every day, because they live in a different state.

Summer is drawing nigh, and it is that time for us to prepare to go back to our hometown to get ready for the beginning of a new school year. We finally returned back to Tennessee. Our mother had a place for us to live. It was a new neighborhood and it was a house. We now live diagonally across the street from our Aunt LuAnn, my mother's sister, and her husband Uncle Dave. They call this part of town, Orange Mound. I am

only seven years old, soon to turn

eight. The next journey for me, started

when we moved on Buntyn Street.

Chapter Twenty
Neighborhood Friends

Being raised on Buntyn Street was a challenge for me. I met new friends in the neighborhood. I met the next-door neighbors who were some live, crunk neighbors, who lived right next door to their kinfolks. The little girl I became close to was, Alicia. My relationship with Alicia became super close. At some point after getting to know Alicia, I wanted to model after her, even though she was only a few weeks younger than I am, she is still a brilliant girl. She is different from everyone else, as I am too. She is about 4'4" has smooth brown skin complexion, long, pretty, black hair, glasses that were thick I couldn't see through them. I didn't make fun of her glasses but I did laugh when her very own cousins would call them, coke bottle glasses. They were just that thick. Overall, she didn't care what you thought about her because she was too busy in the house

studying and completing her

homework assignments, while we

played outside doing nothing. Alicia

is extremely smart in school and she

had the support system from her mom

and dad. She is the kind of girl anyone

would want to model after of. She

lived with her mother, younger sister,

father, and uncle. Her mother is very

sweet, who loved everyone else

children as she loved her very own

children. Everybody's child ran to

Alicia's mother Mrs. Rose. Rose made sure Alicia was educated. She went to a well-known school were the brilliant students attended. Every child wanted to attend White Station but Alicia was bussed to the school because it wasn't in the area.

I attended a private school throughout my years in school. This time around since our move from Whitehaven to Orange Mound and because St. Joseph had closed its doors, I had to attend another private school close by the house. I wasn't going to miss, St. Joseph, because no one liked me anyway. My sister graduated from St. Joseph before they closed their doors. I tried fitting in everywhere I went, but that only lasted for a little while. To me, it seemed as if, no one liked me.

When we moved to our new home, my brother and I attended St. John School around the corner from our home, while our sister Clover attended Bishop Burn across town in the Whitehaven area. She had to catch the city bus to school every morning for her first year of high school. The first time she rode the city bus, she was lost.

My third-grade teacher, how could I ever forget, Ms. Hat! She is tough, stern, and a great teacher. She can appear to be mean because of the look on her face, but she is really a cool and nice teacher, one of the best I've had in school. She's a fun teacher and she knew her math facts. She gave our class multiplication tests. We only had fifteen seconds to solve each one. When she called the multiplication facts out we had to write the answer down and could not solve the problem on paper. Ms. Hat took our class on educational trips. I had never gone to these places before but I do recall going to a restaurant that cooked in front of the crowd. This was a life experience for me. Our Principal is named Notcho. She is unique and different from the other principal at

St. Joseph. Principal Notcho is very interactive and close to the parents and children at the school. She is aware of everything that happens in the school house. Nothing could slip pass Ms. Notcho.

Chapter Twenty-One

Talent and Popularity

My journey into sports and many other things would soon come to flourish. I started playing basketball in the third grade. I played on the junior varsity and varsity team. I am the smallest of them all. Upon playing basketball, I found out that basketball was indeed my sport. I am very good in basketball, as if I've played before. I worked and played hard. I am a very aggressive hustler and ball handler. I knew how to shoot and score points. I am going to follow this dream and continue to play basketball throughout my years of elementary school and beyond.

At St. John, I finally met my cousin everyone had spoken highly of, NaLissa. I knew that NaLissa was my cousin, because she tried to befriend me. NaLissa is a pretty, tall, slender, with that caramel skin tone, and had shoulder length black hair. NaLissa is the eye of them all. She is popular.

NaLissa had a friend name Anna Mae.

NaLissa and Anna Mae were very

close. I recognized how genuine their

friendship is, just by how they

interacted with one another. I tried

fitting in, but it was pretty hard

coping because of the low self-esteem

that was embarked upon me from not

feeling loved. At times, it seemed as if

I was being signal out by everyone

because I was the one having the least

fun. I thought my cousin wasn't

accepting me, so I tried to do whatever it is my cousin wanted me to do, just so I could click up with the popular girls. Remember, I am new to this school, because my old school had closed down. I wanted to look like NaLissa. I am short, chubby, with short sandy brown hair, and still had those pretty hazel eyes, that often changed in color when her mood changed. I was made up more like a butter ball, I felt ashamed of my body. It became hard for me to fit in, it seemed as if I tried too hard and didn't try hard enough. I am different, a lot different than the other girls, and by me being the new kid on the block, it was going to take some most impressive things to fit in the group with my cousin and her crew.

NaLissa started coming over to my Aunt LuAnn house. This became my prime opportunity to get be accepted by NaLissa, after all, we are cousins. NaLissa and I eventually became close and started playing with one another quite frequently. NaLissa had started inviting me over to spend nights at her house. We played all the time and our kinship erupted into us growing up together. We cooked breakfast and it was definitely my favorite, toasted cheese sandwiches.

Chapter Twenty-Two
The P Game

After returning to school, I
became popular too. I was around my
cousin and her crew. I still kind of felt
left out, although they accepted me
under conditions, something still just
didn't seem right. I had on my plaid
skirt, a white oxford button down
shirt; white knee high socks, and
penny loafer shoes. It was the thing to
put pennies or nickels in your penny

loafers, so I had nickels in mine, heads up placed. This was the uniform criteria for the girls that attended St. John School. By the time I entered the fourth grade, I had become well known because of my athletic abilities.

I am a true basketball player and my skills were good. Our school colors were green and white. Each year I played basketball I always wore jersey #'s 24, 10, or 1. Those were my favorite picks. During the next few years at St. John, I became the highest

scorer on the team. I also participated

in cheerleading but I didn't have a

clue to any dance moves, I am stiff as

a straitjacket.

My basketball team held an event

where we played against the parents.

This was a fun event, because we had

a lot of participants and I absolutely

love the game of basketball. My team

was short a player. We had to find

someone to fill in and help us out, so I

had the perfect person, my friend

Draya. She had on a pink jogging suit

and was reluctant to play because she

didn't have the slightest clue of how

to play basketball. And because she

did not know how to play, this was

about to be one hilarious game. Draya

was like an amateur on the floor. We

ran down the court but Draya was still

standing at the opposite end. The

coach was yelling, the parents were

yelling, and because I was the point

guard, I yelled to Draya, "This way

Draya, this way!" Coach Truce called

time out just so she could vaguely

explain to my friend to just run up and

down the court, whichever end the

ball is on, that's the end you go on.

I told her to run up and down the

court whenever she saw everyone else

running. The game resumed. The

parents weren't so bad after all. They

kept up running up and down the floor

but when they were tired, some of

them stopped in the middle of the

game and lied down in the floor

during the middle of the game. We

had a blast and the game turned out to

be successful, better than what we

expected. The game came to an end

because the parents were too tired and

couldn't catch our score. We won

against the parents, 50 -20.

Chapter Twenty-Three

Power

At home, I loved to listen to music. I had a record player that I loved to play all the time. I played my mother's old records. The song I played and danced to all the time was, Tina Turner, "Big Wheel Keep on Rolling." This was her Greatest Hit. I acted out every time I played Tina Turner, feeling like I could play her role and play it well.

My father is a preacher, so it was in my blood to play as a preacher. I practiced sermons that I felt I could one day deliver to a congregation. I did this every day and was moved by the words that came out of my own mouth. There was power behind my voice, something inside of me that stood out when I called myself preaching.

I had a best friend by the name of Shanna. I often spent the weekends with her. Shanna's mother and my mother were very close friends. We were always together. Better yet, I was always with Shanna and her family. Shanna had two sisters. They lived in an apartment complex near Mendenhall on Winchester Rd. We were the best of friends for a few years, until St. John closed down and that's when my best friend and I were separated, which caused our friendship to diminish. I was told that Shanna and her family moved out-of-town. I was now without my best friend. I became very sad, but I knew

that we had to depart, but I had the

slightest clue about how long our

friendship would be compromised.

Chapter Twenty-Four
Class Clown

My brother and his classmates had this one male teacher who was fun but tough on everyone, Mr. Cutthroat. Every single one of us at school loved him even though he is firm and punished you for not taking your education serious, he was still fun to be around. He ran his class like the military. He did not play and he was quick to jack you by your collar,

especially the boys, but he was still
hard on us girls, too.

Danielle is a fast-teenage girl. She
dated Mr. Cutthroat's son. He was at
my cousin house almost every day
after school. Danielle looked for
attention from boys. She wasn't
happy with herself because she didn't
have the body that most of her friends
had, but she had all the material
things that mostly everyone wanted.
She used the material things to buy
love from guys.

Mr. Cut Throat had the hippest class ever. They held an end of the year event with the eighth-grade participation. They performed to the song, "My Girl." I was in competition with a seventh grader, for this boy name Derrick. I really had a crush on him. I knew I was too young for him but that didn't stop my puppy love. Derrick was in the same grade as my cousin Jody. Those eighth and seventh graders wore tuxedos and pretty dresses. They had a great performance. This was the last day for the eighth-grade class.

There was another teacher named Ms. Hillary. She is also my brother's teacher. Major Lee is a class clown. He got away with a lot. One day I went to take something into Ms. Hillary's classroom and my brother and some of his buddies were throwing spit balls in the back of the teacher's hair. She walked with a cane because she had a disability. She is a sweet teacher. She also wore wigs because some of her hair was missing. The day I was in the class, my brother got up and tied a string to the back of Ms. Hillary's wig and tied the other part to the door. As I was collecting the field trip money from Ms. Hillary someone was coming in the classroom, opened the door and what do you know, Ms. Hillary's wig flew off her head. The entire class started laughing aloud. Ms. Hillary tried catching her wig but it was too late. I laughed. She got up and picked her wig up and put it back on her head. She ignored the class and did not entertain what was done to her. I can tell she is kind of embarrassed but sad to say, she was use to the class making fun of her, so she joined in laughing with them. You got me this time, whoever did it, she said to her class.

I had a teacher by the name of Ms. Robins. I didn't like Ms. Robins and she didn't too much care for me either. I gave her a nickname,

"Chicken Legs!" Her legs were made like the drumstick of a chicken. When she walked, she wobbled and her legs rubbed together that every time she wore panty hose, you could hear swoosh-swoosh-swoosh-swoosh. Everyone in the school started calling her by this nickname.

Chapter Twenty-Five

Bullying

I had a classmate named Erica. I was mean to her every day at school. I made sure I sat by her at lunch just so I could take her snacks. I brought my own lunch, but Erica had the good stuff. I didn't realize I was doing what had been done to me, to someone else. I found someone I could pick on that appeared weak to me, to run over. No one ever took my lunch but I was bullied in a lot of other ways. Erica knew that if she didn't give up her snacks freely, I was going to sit as close to her as I could just so I can pinch her until she cried and turned red. I told her that she better not let a tear fall down her face. What I was doing went on for quite some time and no one ever knew about how I was bullying my classmate. This had been going on for a long time that one day, I just knew I was getting Erica's lunch. I didn't bring my lunch this day so I had to go through the lunch line. After I came out the lunch line, I was looking for Erica. I searched for her and finally found her. The teacher tried to tell me to sit somewhere else but I told her I wanted to sit by Erica. Erica looked at me with fear in her eyes. I sat down by her, and carried on as usual. She knew the routine, so I starred at her. I turned my head and said out the side of my mouth, give me that nutty butty. Erica didn't hand over the nutty butty. I said, you better give it to me. Erica said, No! Before you knew it, I had pinched the hell out of Erica. She started crying and went and told the teacher.

What did she do that for? Oh, my goodness, I am in trouble now. I tried thinking of something, not knowing Erica told her mom and her mom had already talked to the teacher about what had been going on. Ms. Robins always tried finding a way to send me to the principal's office and this was one time I was surely going. Ms.

Robins pointed at me and told me to come here. I got up from the cafeteria table nervously, walked over to her and said, yes ma'am! Did you pinch Erica, she asked? Yes ma'am, but she hit me first. No! She didn't, said Ms. Robins. I've been watching you the entire time. Go gather your lunch and go to the office.

I went to the office and was told that I was going to have after school detention and my mother will be called. My mother had to come to a meeting concerning my behavior. I didn't get kicked out but I was being punished for not keeping my hands to myself.

At the time, I didn't feel any remorse for what I did to Erica. Picking on her seemed like my only option because she was my weakest link. Erica is quiet, mild, and meek, and was an easy target for me. Every single day, I was determined to take her lunch and make her feel horrible about herself because I felt horrible about myself.

Erica didn't stand up for herself and she didn't bother anybody but I had to attack someone that I knew is a weak link, like I am. I looked forward to Erica coming to school with her lunch but some days she didn't show up, I was disappointed because I had no one else to pick on. I am cool with everyone and I am cool with Erica, but Erica always brought extra snacks in her lunch. It really wasn't so much as what she had in her lunch, it was

about me being mean to someone who

didn't stand up for themselves. I had

to be mean because people was

always mean to me and treated me the

way I started treating Erica.

Chapter Twenty-Six

Anna and Marcus

My cousin NaLissa was no longer attended St. John. Her mother felt it was best to send her to another school, more for her convenience. NaLissa's buddy Anna Mae was still attending St. John. There was this boy by the name of, Marcus. Marcus was the oldest boy in the school. He was about sixteen years old in the seventh grade. Anna Mae had a thing for

Marcus. I am the look-out girl, after school for these two. Anna Mae didn't know that Marcus wanted me. He tried to get me to feel his penis through his pants but I was too afraid. Anna Mae talked about how big Marcus penis is. I tried hard catching the attention of boys but for some reason they did not pay me any mind. I have a crush on a guy named Derik. He is in the same class with my cousin Jody. Derik is super handsome and had all the girls after him. It is this one girl who liked him, which meant I was in competition to get his attention. Derik acted as if he liked me but I think he was too scared because my cousin and brother attended the same school and always looked after me. Cimon is the other girl who flirted with Derik all the time. I questioned whether they were together or not. Derik flirted with me but he wouldn't take it too far. I had the biggest crush on him, but after so long, that crush soon faded and I eventually moved on.

In the meanwhile, back at home, my mother would get so disgruntle that she would start cursing me and my sister out. She called me out of my name. And I'm not talking about anything nice. I was all kind of low life motherfuckers, a street walker, night-hawk, and was told, I am just like my daddy, no good for nothing. I didn't catch a break from the name calling. I can't figure out what I had did so bad, to be called the lowest of

all, from my own biological mother,

but this is the life I am faced with, at

home. My mother is so mean towards

me and my sister. I never saw her

treat my brother the way she treated

her daughters.

I developed this complex about

myself, I developed low self-esteem,

felt worthless, and always thought

that no one liked or loved me. I am

faced with brutality of the unwanted. I

did everything to be accepted and I

tried to please my mother, but she never embraced that I needed to feel love from her.

How could this happen? How could my mother feel so ill about her own daughters? What did my sister and I do, for our mother to be so mean to us? I didn't know the answer to these questions in my head and as time went on, it only became worse.

I tried everything to please my mother, but it seemed that no matter what I did, it still wasn't good enough for her. But that didn't stop my mother from calling me out of my name. No matter what I did, whether right or wrong, according to my mother, I was always going to be wrong, in her eyesight. I couldn't make my mother happy no matter what. She is just too damn mean and hateful to me. I was too young to understand why my mother was so mean and hateful towards me.

St. John usually remained opened, but the upcoming year, the school was going to close down due to financial problems and low attendance. This meant that I had to attend another school for my last year in elementary. When school starts back next year in September, I will be promoted to the eighth grade going to a brand-new school. I wanted to attend the school my neighborhood friends went to, but my mom and this traditional stuff she had to follow, she was keeping me in a private school.

Chapter Twenty-Seven

My Father's New Family

My father is very supportive when it came to my activities at school. He had remarried to a woman that is very nice and treated us as her own. He had two children, Major III and Christian, with his new wife. My brother Major III was only a few years younger than me, which further let me know the reason my father had done such terrible things of kicking us out and becoming overly aggressive towards my mom. He was cheating and it finally came to the light.

We called my father's new wife, Momma Cherl. She had three daughters, Aarushi, Abagail, and Abbie, from a previous relationship. She moved in the house, that we once called home. Me, my brother Major, and sister Clover visited quite often, but shortly after, Major and Clover stopped going over to our father's house.

I loved going over my father's house. I wanted to live with him, but was too afraid to leave my mentally and verbally abusive mother, because I also loved my mother even though she didn't show me the affection I was yearning for, from her. I was torn between my father and mother. There wasn't anything my father wouldn't do for me. After all, he was the one who attended my games and was always there for me. He was my

protector. I am truly a daddy's girl.

Momma Cherl and her daughters

were very welcoming. We all got

along well. Aarushi was the one who

cooked all the time. I recall my big

sister calling us in the kitchen to some

caramel popcorn that she had created.

It was so delicious!! Every time I

visited my father, I asked my sister

Aarushi, to pop me that special

popcorn she could make.

As time went on, the family became closer. My sister Abagail was still living at home. She was the baby girl out of her, Aarushi and Abbie. I hung around Abagail in the downstairs room where she slept. I always found myself walking with her over to her friend guy house from time to time. Abagail shared a secret with me. I received the devastating news but kept quiet about it. Our other sister Clover had experienced the same thing that Abagail had shared with me. What I didn't understand is how my father could sexually assault his own daughters. This couldn't be, I thought! Did my father really do the same thing to my sister Abagail the same thing he did to my sister Clover? Was Abagail talking about my father or some other man her mom had previously been in a relationship with? It was too much for me to process, but one thing I knew is that I had to protect my big sisters and keep watch on them.

Abagail is frightened and terrified. She stayed locked her room dreading the fact that it may happen to her again. No one understood her pain, but I did. Momma Cherl didn't realize the devastating situation she had now put her own daughter in. Did Momma Cherl care? Or was she just another wife whose very own daughter became a victim to rape by the man she married and loved?

Abagail dealt with her pain, the best way she knew how, and that was to now play the role as being a grown woman in a teenager's body. This very act caused her to have doubts and not trust anyone. She was just another victim and was preyed upon by a sick minded individual who played the role as her father. Abagail is very sweet, kind, and cheerful. By just looking at her, you wouldn't have known she had been taken advantage of by a grown ass man that was supposed to protect, love, and take care of her, not take advantage of her.

She kept a smile on her face despite the devastating event that took place in her life.

Clover and Abagail were now in the same predicament. They both were quiet individuals who did not bother anyone but was blamed for something that they had no control over. They felt unwanted and unloved. How could they deal with the position they were put in?

Why did our mothers not press charges? Why did they continue to let this happen to their daughters? Were

they threatened by my father? Were

they too afraid to speak out? Did they

feel that it would all be alright and

would pass over soon? Did this very

same thing that was done to their

daughters, was it done to them?

Many questions plagued my mind. I

couldn't understand for the life of me

why a mother would allow something

to continue to go on and not have this

man locked up. I thought parents were

meant to protect their children, not

harm them or put them in harm's way.

I found myself closer to my sisters

Clover and Abagail. I understood

molestation all too well because I am

also a victim of molestation. I tried to

figure out how I could continue to

stay close to my sisters. I feel it is my

duty to try and protect them since no

one else has. This is too much for me

to digest at one time. I am in disbelief.

No way possible this could have

happened, I thought to myself. I loved

my father and I didn't think less about

him, but clearly if he did this to my

sisters, it is wrong and unjustifiable.

My sisters deserved to be protected. I

love everyone and I just want

everyone to get along.

Chapter Twenty-Eight

To Be Continued

It appeared that everyone left me to the point where I started feeling worthless. I was thriving to be noticed by my very own mother, but she didn't care. I wanted to be accepted, and because of this, things started shifting in my life….

You're thinking about your life and the challenges you've faced, huh? Unleashed Chains is meant to bring you the naked truth about a southern girl who ran into obstacles everywhere she turned. Sandy wanted out of every situation but she wasn't taught how to break free because her mother was bound by her own deceiving mind. The Generational curses were passed on to her but she is determined to find her way through to get out of these

taunting situations.

Find out some more about how

Sandy coped with her best friend

moving away and the many other

challenges she faced in her life, in

volume 2 of Unleashed Chains.